T0265776

PRAISE FOR **CHAD PRINKEY** AND
WELL BUILT

Leading a construction company through turbulent, complicated times like ours is challenging. *Well Built* is an actionable playbook on how to do it well. This is a must-read for
any current or aspiring construction executive.

—Kevin Rogge
President, Harvey-Cleary Builders

Well Built is a game-changer for construction business owners
and executives seeking lasting prosperity. This book is a
blueprint for excellence, providing a strategic approach that
will help you build an action plan to ensure your construction business thrives. We have considered Chad a partner to
our business for a long time, and I would urge you not to
miss out on the wisdom that has in-part fueled our success.

—Frank Settleman
President, Chesapeake Contracting Group

Having had the privilege of collaborating with Chad Prinkey
during his tenure with our company as a consultant, I can
attest firsthand to his profound insights into effective leader-

ship. In his new book, *Well Built*, Chad Prinkey distills years of hands-on experience and strategic wisdom into a comprehensive guide for aspiring and established leaders alike.

—Buddy Henley
LEED AP, BD+C; President, Henley Construction Co., Inc.

Chad Prinkey's *Well Built: How the Top 2% of Construction Contractors Create Superior Value, Profits, and Excellence* is a game-changer for the industry. His insights have helped me build the competitive edge needed for success. Prinkey's guidance equips contractors with the strategies and mindset necessary to transform their construction business. This book is a blueprint for excellence, empowering leaders to thrive and stand out in an ever-competitive landscape. It is a must-read for those committed to achieving remarkable results.

—Aaron Shapiro
Business Development Manager, Shapiro & Duncan, Inc.

I discovered Chad through his efforts to create content to help improve GC-subcontractor relations. His advocacy for creating a healthier environment for everyone by working on the root causes of industry dysfunction was refreshing and caught my attention immediately. We work closely with Chad and his team to help Contexture deliver customer delight without sacrificing our business objectives. The construction industry needs more voices like his.

—Brianna Goodwin
President & CEO, Contexture

Strong leaders show the path forward and inspire people to become the best version of themselves. They also have the courage and conviction to challenge the status quo and stand for positive change. Chad has risen to his position as a sought-after consultant and thought leader in the construction industry by doing both of these things consistently. His book, *Well Built*, provides clear, inspirational, and actionable advice for General Contractors and Trade Contractors. The message is right on target for the needs of today's construction industry.

—Jason E. Keller
Managing Partner, Block Companies

As a multigenerational mechanical contractor with multiple locations, we were seeking a systematic way to run our business into the future. We read [other books on the subject] and loved the framework but wanted someone who deeply understood contractors to help facilitate the essential business decisions we needed to make. We've found the systematic approach Chad has taken with our team to mesh nicely with concepts with EOS to drive real results for us. In *Well Built*, Chad brings answers to questions facing contractors who want to create a more sustainable business.

—Dominic D. Magnolia
Vice President, Magnolia Companies

Chad inspires construction leaders wherever he goes, which I've experienced firsthand in his work with our team. When he speaks at trade association events, they are consistently the best-attended and reviewed events of the year. We've considered him a trusted partner to our business for years, and through that partnership, we've become a larger, more effective, and more profitable business. Chad's in-depth experience with so many contractors has given him an extremely well-rounded and valuable perspective on common challenges and best practices from around the industry. *Well Built* is clearly a culmination of the principles we've found so influential over the years, and every commercial construction leader should keep a copy on hand.

—Evan Winston
President, Hercules Fence

We first met Chad as a speaker at an industry conference and found his insights to be right on target with the realities facing trade contractors. His team has been delivering excellent results for our company ever since! We especially appreciate his perspective from working with general contractors and developers to help us understand what our clients need from us. *Well Built* organizes Chad's insights into a guide we can follow to create consistent success in our business.

—Mark Huntley
Principal, Anchor Mechanical

Chad Prinkey's *Well Built* provides construction companies with an actionable blueprint for success. Chad's years of experience as a consultant to construction firms have lent him the expertise and perspective to identify what smart companies need to do to build winning teams, run profitable projects, and skillfully manage risk. From my personal experience in working closely with Chad, leaders seeking to grow their firms won't want to miss this thoughtful guide.

—Steve Houff

President, Plano-Coudon Construction

Chad has done a lot of work in our industry with a lot of companies. We truly value his knowledge, insight and instincts.

—Scott Harding

President & CEO, FB Harding Electrical Contractors

WELL BUILT

CHAD PRINKEY

WELL BUILT

HOW THE TOP 2% OF

CONSTRUCTION CONTRACTORS

CREATE SUPERIOR VALUE,

PROFITS, AND EXCELLENCE

Advantage | Books

Published by Advantage Books, Charleston, South Carolina.
An imprint of Advantage Media.

ADVANTAGE is a registered trademark, and the Advantage colophon is a trademark of Advantage Media Group, Inc.

Printed in the United States of America.

10 9 8 7 6 5 4 3 2 1

ISBN: 979-8-89188-060-3 (Paperback)
ISBN: 979-8-89188-059-7 (Hardcover)
ISBN: 979-8-89188-061-0 (eBook)

Library of Congress Control Number: 2024904296

Cover design by Megan Elger.
Layout design by Analisa Smith.

This publication is designed to provide accurate and authoritative information in regard to the subject matter covered. It is sold with the understanding that the publisher is not engaged in rendering legal, accounting, or other professional services. If legal advice or other expert assistance is required, the services of a competent professional person should be sought.

Advantage Books is an imprint of Advantage Media Group. Advantage Media helps busy entrepreneurs, CEOs, and leaders write and publish a book to grow their business and become the authority in their field. Advantage authors comprise an exclusive community of industry professionals, idea-makers, and thought leaders. For more information go to **advantagemedia.com**.

*To the builders of construction companies that create jobs for
people to do honest work they can be proud of.*

CONTENTS

Well Built Construction Companies

Our Audience

Those with the dreams and willingness to invest in enhancing the physical space around us have created amazing spaces for us to enjoy and an industry that happily and gainfully employs millions of people yearly. Construction companies deserve our appreciation for helping to build the world we enjoy today. Construction project owners and designers deserve our gratitude for dreaming up those new and better spaces. Throughout this book, I'll be using the term *construction companies* about the audience I'm trying to reach. That audience primarily consists of general and specialty contractors, specifically executives and rising leaders within those firms. A&E (architecture and engineering) firms may also derive value from the content of this book, as their environments are not so dissimilar. As contractors take a deeper interest in design/build, the lines between A&E and construction blur. Owners are the people these construction companies exist to service. Developers, property owners, tenants, governmental agencies, institutions (schools, hospitals, etc.), and even homeowners are considered owners.

In this context, I'll reference *owners* throughout the book, but it is not written for them as an audience. Other companies exist to fuel the work of the construction companies that deserve consideration and are mentioned throughout the book but that don't fall into the category of construction companies in this writing. Those companies include construction materials manufacturers, construction equipment manufacturers, and suppliers and dealers of both.

While it's not written for them, I hope many are reading as, being pulled by the ebbs and flows of the capital projects market themselves, many concepts herein will apply to their businesses. It may help them better serve many of their clients, the contractors for whom the book is written.

Industry Challenges

Construction is a tough business. The companies operating in this industry must learn to manage adversity. Here's an admittedly inadequate list of the challenges I see in the industry. To allow you the additional space to complain, I contemplated leaving three blank pages after this brief list so you can add your own list!

1. Economic factors cause feast-or-famine conditions regularly, so in the good times, there is a constant fear of taking on too much overhead to survive in the lean times. Most contractors have made layoffs at one point or another, and many are gun-shy about growth as a result.

2. Margins are lean for everyone involved, even in good times. The competition created around low-bid procurement in the industry has ensured that.

3. Multiple-bid-procurement methods abound, and the low price wins the day most of the time.

4. Less-than-scrupulous construction companies will underbid projects to rack up profits through unplanned billings via change orders on the project.

5. Construction design is an imperfect thing, and the adoption of virtual design and construction (VDC) to achieve more accuracy is spotty. The more complex the industry becomes, the harder it is to nail a perfect design before the project begins. There is much finger-pointing when something in the design must be changed in the field. There's little room for favors between construction companies and owners.

6. Companies that work hard to provide a better experience for their customers and employees are rarely rewarded for the effort with more work unless they're cheaper. As a result, many construction companies are not committed to providing a consistently positive customer or employee experience.

7. Not enough young people are choosing the construction industry. Companies struggle to find people to recruit and fill office and field roles daily.

8. Large segments of the industry are highly dependent on an undocumented immigrant field-labor force, which operates in a shadow economy rife with bad actors. In some geo-graphic regions and types of construction, if you're not using

undocumented labor, you can't compete. Meanwhile, it is illegal to hire these workers directly, so shady labor brokers take on that risk and act as subcontractors.

9. Relative to other industries, construction companies don't market themselves well, if at all. This contributes to the lack of people finding and entering the industry.

10. The average contractor is a small business. These small businesses with tight margins tend not to have the wherewithal to reinvest enough into their businesses in the form of technology, staff, and training.

11. The construction industry has lagged behind almost all other industries in terms of innovation and improved productivity, so we're doing things today essentially the same way we've been doing them for five decades and counting.

The Top 2 Percent

The companies managing this adversity effectively and thriving despite these realities are beating the odds. The average GC/CM earns net profits of around 1.5 percent yearly, and the average specialty contractor is around 6 percent yearly. However, a small group of high-performance construction companies consistently perform at more than three times the average profit statistics, with only minor dips tied to economic conditions. These companies are not only achieving a high net-profit percentage—it is much easier to drive a strong net-profit percentage as a very small contractor with very low overhead—but being in the middle of their respective construction markets or larger, the top 2 percent are also generating millions of dollars of net profit. My experience with the market suggests that the number of unusually high net-profit mid-to-large construction companies is about one in fifty. I've worked personally as an advisor to nearly two hundred construction companies over the past fifteen years. Their hiring of a consultant immediately puts them in a class of companies just like yours that are committed to improvement, which is a trait of top performers. Therefore, many of the companies I've been fortunate enough to work with were already top performers before our engagement, perhaps one in four. With that in mind, I've had in-depth exposure to roughly fifty top-2-percent construction companies and played a role in creating many more.

WBCC Pyramid

2% WBCC: Running uncommonly successful businesses following the practices in this book.

48% of Contractors: Want to be their best, but struggle with industry norms.

50% of Contractors: Disinterested in being a "great" company. Lifestyle businesses.

What do these top-2-percent contractors have in common? They're not all the largest companies, though many are market leaders. Plenty of large construction companies are just eking out a profit every year, so sheer size is not the measure of success for the one in fifty I'm talking about. They're not all in a specific geographical market or trade. Our focus in the pages ahead is what ties these top 2 percent of contractors together. They share a common set of operating principles that consistently leads to top performance. We've organized those principles into a system you can learn and implement to get the same results.

Our Purpose in Writing

I founded a consulting firm, Well Built Construction Consulting, with the specific intention of helping ambitious construction companies to implement these principles to become better businesses. We systematically assess the current states of our client companies against the principles of the top 2 percent and coach them to implement each principle on a prioritized timeline. Our team consists of construction industry experts passionate about improving the lives of the great people who have chosen to dedicate their careers to building the world around us. To make our consulting work more efficient, we organized the principles of the top 2 percent into a system that works much like a checklist for our engagements. Our clients have enjoyed incredible success, measured in improved profits, higher employee satisfaction, awards for quality and safety, and sustained growth through various market conditions.

This book aims to share those principles with you in the same systematic format used by the team of consultants at Well Built Construction Consulting so you can learn them and implement them yourself. In this writing, I've focused on (1) simple clarity, and (2) your ability to put these principles into action in your construction business. If you are inspired to implement the system but find you cannot do it yourself, we are here to help, so use the contact information provided with this book to reach out if needed.

Some Disclaimers

This book isn't for everyone. If you're a company that thrives on the dysfunction in the industry and wants to maintain the status quo, this isn't for you. If you're a contractor who enjoys bidding work lower than it can be performed, as you bank on inconsistencies in the plans to give you a chance to change-order your way to a better margin, the ideas I set forth for building an *ethical* and profitable construction company are probably not for you. If you're a general contractor that enjoys underbidding your trades, banking on your ability to strongarm subs into your budget downstream, you'll hate reading about the necessity to stop that corrosive behavior. If you are that kind of company today and no longer want to be, however, this book could be for you, and it might just change your company and your life forever.

To glean value from reading this book, you must be committed to improvement. You'll need a flexible mindset and a willingness to change. You must value the humans inside your company, clients, subs, and suppliers. You must want to improve your company and the industry and be willing to embrace strong ethics. The principles I'll share aren't cheats or hacks. They will take discipline to apply, and if the statements above don't fit you, you'll have a hard time making the philosophical switch to this new way of thinking and working.

These principles will be introduced systematically and should be applied in order. If you take that approach, capture the most salient points in a notebook as you read or listen along. If you'd rather pick and choose what makes sense to you, there's still value laid out in these pages, but I encourage you to go all in and become a Well Built Construction Company (WBCC). The book follows the WBCC System, which is made up of six subsystems in its optimal order of implementation into your business.

I use the terms *GC* and *CM* interchangeably throughout. I'm referring to the company the owner hires to handle construction on their behalf, and as contract types and delivery methods are not in the scope of the WBCC System, please don't let that distinction bother you.

I also use the terms *specialty contractor*, *trade contractor*, and *subcontractor* interchangeably throughout. While I speak about them as subcontractors only in the context of being hired by a GC, you may feel compelled to correct me occasionally. If so, I'm sorry in advance. Contractors in the field putting work in place are the heartbeat of construction, and I would never intentionally disparage them.

Finally, this system isn't magic. I don't even think of it as mine. I merely capture and bring order to my observations about top-performing construction companies. For fifteen years, my role has been to work alongside amazing construction companies as a partner to help them meet their goals. I've never woken up in the places of the owners, executives, and managers I've coached, so my perspective is always that of an inside outsider. I'm inside, in that I am deeply a part of the construction industry, but I'm outside because I don't lead a construction business myself. I lead a consulting business. Remember that as you read, and if you disagree with the system I'll present in the pages ahead, maybe your experience is different from the one-hundred-plus contractors I've helped. That is an admittedly small cross-section of our industry. If your experience differs, I would love feedback about where you disagree so I can learn from you to enhance future editions of this book!

OK, let's roll. I am confident that your choice to become a WBCC will enrich you professionally and personally while making the construction industry a better place for all of us. Cheers!

Installing the Foundation

T hroughout this book, you will encounter many ideas for how to improve your construction company. You may even be inspired to act. I certainly hope so! With that said, assuming you're operating a construction company today as opposed to thinking of starting one up, there's no way you should apply these ideas to your business beyond the Foundation chapter until all its elements are in place. If, as you work through the Foundation, you find you have each element soundly operating as I describe (or better!), I hope you'll feel satisfied and reassured to read that you are doing things the right way. But even if you're sure your foundation is strong, don't skip this section. If you are a reader choosing to arm yourself with the knowledge from this book before starting your company, however, it would make more sense to start your work with System II: Engineering a Clear Strategic Direction. Without a business to manage today, the most important thing for you is to decide what you wish to become. Then, come right back to the Foundation and prioritize the recommendations from this chapter.

The Foundation is a set of vital information and habits of success that every contractor should have in place. If you're missing any piece of the Foundation, you aren't ready to address any other area of your business. The chapters show customization for both general contractors and specialty contractors. If you feel there is something about your specific business not adequately covered in the Foundation, please contact us at booksupport@wellbuiltconsulting.com, and we'll walk you through it.

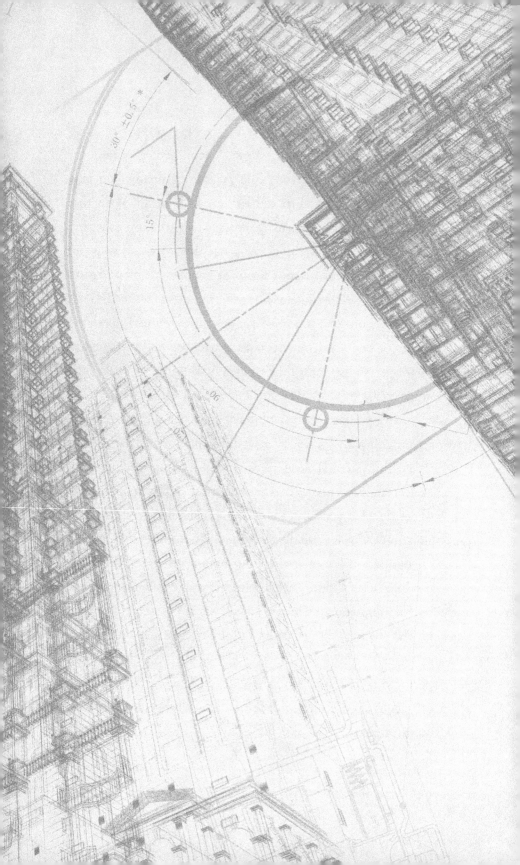

CHAPTER 1

Financial Transparency

As you may know, construction is a relatively low-profit margin business compared to other industries. In my experience and research into various industry benchmarking tools, even the top 2 percent of companies are specialty contractors who average 12 to 15 percent and might rarely peak at over 20 percent net profit. In comparison, the top-performing general contractors can only hope to achieve something close to 5 to 8 percent net. Some extremely specialized contractors will be exceptions to these averages, but construction is not like software, banking, or commercial real estate, with average net profits well into the 20-percent-plus range. This means strong financial management is especially important to contractors, and the lack of margin makes it a matter of life and death.

The owner of one midsize specialty contractor (about $20 million) always relied on others to manage his company's finances. He was a tradesman and an entrepreneur, not an accountant, so he paid others to know that information. At the end of the year, he was never thrilled with what he had left over, but he made peace with it and kept pushing harder the next year. His trusted controller presented the financials reliably by the fifteenth of every month and presented a simple picture the owner could understand. It worked this way for twenty years. One day, the controller was injured in a bad car accident and kept out of the office for six months of intense recovery.

Through their trusted network of other contractors, they found an outsourced CFO to take the reins in the interim. After a month in the role, the outsourced CFO found a disturbing pattern of funds being shifted from the company each month to outside bank accounts. The amounts were each small enough—$10,000 here and $8,000 there—to not have caught much attention. The pattern stretched back over fifteen years. The controller had stolen nearly $2 million from an unsuspecting owner for over a decade. When the controller left the hospital, they went to prison, where they sit today.

Many of you know of a similar story. The moral of the story is to be an owner who knows how your finances work.

How Contractors Die

The top reason contractors go out of business is the continued negative cash flow. However, this is only the symptom, not the disease. The reason contractors experience continued negative cash flow varies. It could be a lack of sales combined with carrying too much overhead. It could also be owners pulling too much money out of the business, leaving the company with limited cash reserves to weather difficult times. The most common reason is taking on more work than they can handle, failing to meet their contractual obligations, having payment withheld, and defaulting with subs and vendors. Many big-name contractors have met their ends in this way.

There's an even more pervasive issue causing construction companies to fail than the examples listed above. This reason is not as flashy, and the results don't make headlines. It is the fundamental lack of timely, clear financial information or failure to understand the swift corrective action necessary based on the information. That lack of information and lack of reacting to it is rampant across the construction industry and puts contractors out of business more than any other issue. It often leads to contractors ending up in negative cash flow positions, so that's the reason most cited. Owing to the small size of the average contractor, owners' backgrounds in the trades and engineering rather than accounting and finance, and thin margins offering limited room for adding professional accounting overhead, far too many contractors do not have full transparency into their financial situations. When our consulting firm is hired to help a client realize their vision for their company, all their hopes and dreams are on pause if they don't have their financial house in order from the start. If any of the following is not transparent, we cannot move forward with any other business improvement initiatives until we have a resolution:

- Accurate work-in-progress (WIP) reports for the previous month

- Backlog visibility with resource-loading projections, showing the ability to staff work already under contract

- Accurate monthly P&L reporting for the previous month

- Accurate balance sheet reporting for the previous month

I hope you're reviewing this list and thinking, *No problem.* If you're not, this is now your top priority to address in your business. A good accountant with a strong construction background can help get any of these things in place. There are also resources like the Construction Financial Management Association (CFMA) that offer training and certification programs for you and your people. I encourage all company owners and executives to undergo extensive training to become fluent in the financial language of their businesses. You will not regret the time spent learning how to manage the lifeblood of your business.

CHAPTER 2

Financial Roadblocks

Bad WIP

WIP problems are the most common. It's because nonaccounting people must be relied upon to perform key functions that contribute to the timeliness and accuracy of the metrics. Efforts must be made on all sides to succeed with accurate data entry from field and office project personnel. Employees must commit to meeting the expected standards of data entry. No excuses. Having the right information about what we're spending on employee time and materials on every project, no matter what, is not a nice to have. It's a must. So it is necessary to have managers who set clear standards and hold people accountable. Nobody loves tracking and reporting, but it is not hindering you from doing your job; it's a vital part of your job. To gain the most accurate picture possible, you should even have your project managers and estimators track their time against projects, using "cost codes" relevant to their departments.

The company should do everything possible to reduce friction caused by complicated or user-unfriendly systems. Financial software should be updated regularly enough to capitalize on technological advances that create better user experiences and efficiency. I've seen this play out many times, and the software upgrades are almost always worth it. The company must also provide regular training on the tools and test every employee to ensure they know what they're expected to do with the software. Too many employees are unsure of how to use tools vital to company success. Also, erring on the side of fewer, less complicated tracking requirements is wise. If you have forty cost codes for the same thing, don't be surprised when you can't figure out the facts.

Knowing what to do with the WIP information once you have it is another set of skills entirely. First, let's talk about percentage complete compared to percentage billed and spent. The percentage complete requires the experience and judgment of someone on your team who has walked the project and compared the work in place versus the total scope of the project. This should be tracked weekly to ensure progress compared to the schedule, but the data should also be updated in the WIP report for comparison to the costs incurred to date, the amount billed to date, and the percentage complete. You hope to see that your billings are right on pace with the work in place and costs are on or under pace. For example, on a $10 million project, we have assessed it at 50 percent complete. We've billed $5 million (50 percent) and spent $3.5 million on a total budget of $8 million (43.75 percent). This project is on track to succeed, and we even have some wiggle room in our costs.

WIP Example					
Project	**Contract Value**	**Estimated Cost**	**Cost to Date**	**Billings to Date**	**+/-**
Project A	$1,000,000	$750,000	$650,000 (87% spent)	$900,000 (90% billed)	$30,000 (3% over billed)
Project B	$2,000,000	$1,400,000	$1,000,000 (71% spent)	$1,420,000 (71% billed)	0

Actual % complete must come from professional assessment and breakdown of projected costs to complete. If we're 90% complete on Project A, we will beat profit projections!

Sometimes you are underbilled. That means you have billed for less than the percentage complete. Underbillings are technically an asset in accounting-speak because you are theoretically still owed the balance of what you haven't billed. If you are following the best practice of having a capable member of your team conducting weekly site walks and producing their view of percentage complete, this may be the case, and your team just needs to get some billings caught up!

However, more commonly, underbillings aren't a result of your team failing to bill in accordance with the work in place. Instead, you aren't following the best practice of assessing percentage complete, and you're relying instead on your costs to date to indicate percentage complete. Using this all-too-common method, you assume (remember the adage about assumptions?) that if we have spent 50 percent of our budget, we must be 50 percent of the way through the project, and all we need to do is get our billings up from 40 to 50 percent, and we'll be on track, right? Too often, you haven't put 50 percent of the work in place, or you would have billed for it. Instead, you are 40 percent complete, and the problem isn't billings; it's that you're blowing your budget on something, and you need to find out what—and in a hurry.

Other times you are overbilled. That is, you've billed for more than the percentage complete. Using the same comparison to your costs, overbillings are usually a good sign that you're spending less and completing more. Otherwise, you wouldn't have billed for it. Again, the best practice of developing a real percentage-complete estimate to compare with the actual billings and costs to date will help bring clarity to the issue.

Delayed Payment

Behind getting the WIP in order, the other most common financial roadblock is delayed payment. There are four strategies for overcoming this roadblock.

First, submit all invoices on time, and confirm within days they have been approved. I can't tell you how many times I've seen payment held inexplicably for 120 or more days, only to find out there was a problem with the invoice back when it was originally submitted. The fix often takes only minutes, and much needed cash flow is forthcoming.

Second, maintain a rigorous process for tracking and following up with open invoices. From the time the invoice is one day past due, your team should be aware and act in a structured way. I recommend an email and phone call combination every fifteen to thirty days from the time an invoice is late, with official letters going out at sixty-plus days late—attorneys by ninety. Phone calls should be made to accounting contacts and decision-maker contacts with your clients who can help move things along. Calling and asking for your money is never fun and can feel embarrassing, but getting into an urgent cash flow situation is much more embarrassing still.

The third is mastering documentation. Change orders are the biggest culprit here. Whether you're a GC or a sub, getting paid on change orders by the owner is necessary for most projects. I wish it weren't so, but that's a topic for another book. Subcontractors should establish a standard of backup beyond reproach by even the most discerning GCs and owners. Pictures, details, and support from notable industry reference guides will usually do the trick. Most GCs have no interest in holding up your change order requests, but they do have a fiduciary responsibility to their clients to evaluate them thoroughly. General contractors should have in-depth expectation-setting discussions with the owner and their subcontractors about what standard of backup will be required from the start of a project. A great GC should educate owners and subs alike on navigating this contentious issue gracefully and empathetically.

Fourth is the strategy of front-loading the schedule of values to get positive cash flow going. This is particularly important for self-performing contractors shouldering labor and materials costs throughout construction. Getting money in the door quickly is directly tied to your billings. If you're not billing enough early on, even when you get paid, it won't be enough to stay in the black. This strategy must be executed ethically and responsibly to avoid creating mistrust, but nobody benefits from a contractor going broke in the middle of construction, so for the good of the project, take the steps to get ahead of the game financially.

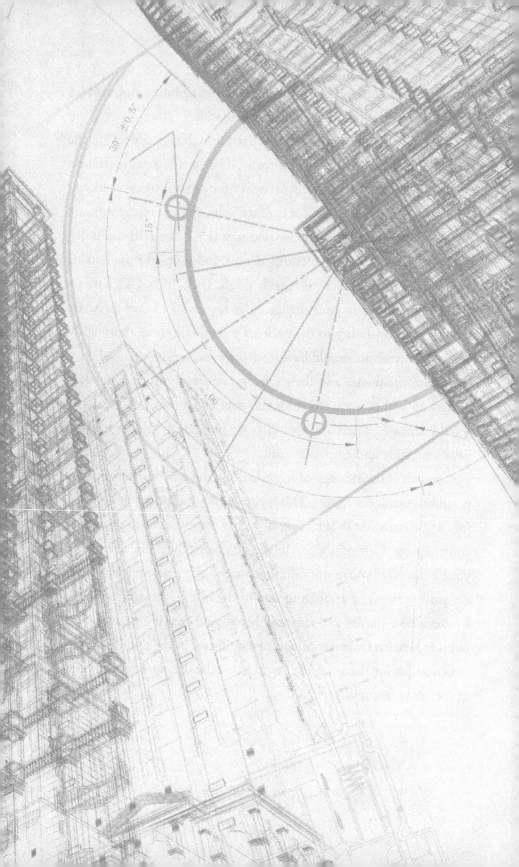

CHAPTER 3

Measure What Matters and Make a Profit

Leading Indicators

Most people have had some personal experience with personal weight goals at one point in their life or another. If you haven't, the following analogy will still make sense, even if it lacks the personal and emotional triggers it has for me and the rest of us who have wrestled with our weight occasionally.

For weight goals, the ultimate measure of your success or failure is provided by a tool most of us will find sitting on our bathroom floor. The scale doesn't lie, as they say. You step on, and whatever that number says, it is what it is, and there's nothing you can do about it while you're standing there. That number, the measure of your weight in pounds (or kilograms for our metric friends), is what is known as a lagging indicator.

A lagging indicator is a measure of a result. Lagging indicators are the things that most people focus on because they're looking for results in their lives. We want to achieve a certain weight, make a certain amount of money, or shoot a certain golf score and obsess over these success measures. These are all lagging indicators. The results are downstream of decisions we made along the way.

We can't simply want to lose weight and change nothing in our lives, expecting a different outcome. What should we do if we want the number on our scale to change? The answer is plain. We must address our life choices, chiefly our diet and exercise choices. If we shift our focus from the number on the scale to the foods we choose, we'll impact the number on that scale. To succeed with your weight goals, establish a plan for diet and exercise (and other things, depending on the plan you're using) that maps to your target weight, then follow the plan. You may use tools to help you follow the plan by measuring your actions. You can download an app to log all your meals, wear a smartwatch to track your exercise and calorie burn, and publish your daily progress in a group with your healthy friends on social media. This kind of behavior is proven to create lasting results, and while it takes hard work, it's not a complex concept. Determine a goal, build a well-informed plan for meeting the goal, and track your actions to ensure you're following the plan. Poof! Goal attainment.

Focusing on your actions rather than the outcomes you want has another significant psychological benefit. If you redefine success daily away from what the scale says and toward following the plan, you can win every single day because following the plan is 100 percent within your control. This leads to a daily sense of accomplishment that can be used as fuel to maintain daily momentum. But if your only definition of success is what that scale says, it can be difficult to maintain your momentum because you can't win every day when, by your own definition, winning can only occur once you've achieved your outcome.

In our analogy, diet and exercise are known as leading indicators, which means they are the factors that, done successfully, lead to your target outcomes. The best leading indicators are action-based because action-based things put you in full control. With very few extreme exceptions, nobody can force you to eat in a way different from your plan or keep you from exercising today. Those are your choices, and while there can be obstacles to following your plan, you're in direct control and can overcome those obstacles.

Let's tie all this in. WBCCs know that any outcome they want to drive in their business must be reverse-engineered to focus on the action-based plan to create that outcome. They then measure those actions, knowing that the way to achieve an outcome is to do the right things. If you're like most construction companies, you're not measuring enough things in your business, and you're probably measuring almost only lagging indicators. In a construction company, net profit is the ultimate lagging indicator, and the number matters most to your company's current health. Let's break net profit down into some of its leading indicators to help you evaluate what you should measure. Please remember I am not an accountant, and this is not an accounting book, so the following is not intended to be a granular construction accounting exercise.

1. **Gross profit.** The amount of money left over after paying for direct, project-related costs. Gross profit is perhaps the most important measure of a construction company's potential to achieve strong net profits. There should be a gross profit goal for the company, for each profit center, and for every project. Achieving strong gross profit is tied to estimating projects accurately, running them efficiently, and making enough total revenue to generate the overall pool of gross profit needed. *Note: For self-performing contractors, one of the*

most useful metrics is gross profit per man hour—that means the amount of gross profit allocated to every hour your workforce was on a job. Projects with low GP/MH soak up all your potential labor for very little return, while high GP/MH jobs provide a great return on your labor.

2. **Overhead.** These are non-production-related business expenses that must be paid out of your gross profit. These expenses are often called SG&A (selling, general, and administrative expenses) and encapsulate virtually every dollar you're spending that cannot be attributed to the cost of running your projects directly. All those project-related costs, remember, should be accounted for line by line in your estimates. Overhead must be budgeted and managed to ensure your business doesn't outspend its gross profits.

3. **Total revenue.** While the goal of a WBCC is never tied only to its revenue (for them, revenue is vanity, while profit is sanity), the total revenue number is an important measure because the costs to run the business must be covered by a sufficient sum of money to generate that gross profit, which is used to cover all overhead. For example, if I want a net profit of $1 million and have an overhead of $2.5 million, then I know I need a gross profit of $3.5 million to hit my net profit goal. If my goal for gross profit on my projects is 20 percent, then I need to target a total revenue goal of $17.5 million. Without getting into accounting minutiae (that I'm unqualified to do in the first place), that's $17.5 million in revenue.

4. **Backlog.** The work for which you have signed contracts but has not yet been completed falls into the backlog category. Construction is a project-based business in that the things

you're working on today will end in a finite period, and there must be something else for you to work on afterward. You can have an incredibly busy month followed by a period of layoffs. Companies that don't keep their eye on the backlog can become surprised by a drop-off in work that turns their labor force into unplanned overhead because they don't have projects to work on. Looking at the total backlog can also be misleading. You must also consider when the work in your backlog will be performed. Having a large backlog that starts eight months from now doesn't help you next month!

5. **Pipeline.** Projects that a company is pursuing through bidding or budgeting but may not be awarded make up the pipeline. Tracking backlog is important, but too few construction companies effectively track the potential projects that will eventually make up the backlog. Well Built Construction Companies monitor their pipelines and keep a good handle on their conversion rate from pipeline to backlog. This tells them how much qualified work they need to estimate to provide enough pipeline to achieve their backlog and, eventually, their revenue goals.

6. **Employee satisfaction.** That's right—this is something to be measured just like any other metric. There is a direct correlation between low employee turnover and strong gross profit. There is another direct correlation between happy employees and low turnover. So one of the key things Well Built Construction Companies know they must measure is the satisfaction of their employee base. They do this through both formal and informal methods. Employee engagement surveys, exit interview feedback, and candid one-on-one

chats with mentors and managers provide companies with the information they need to maintain a happy workforce that stays and does their best work.

7. **Customer satisfaction.** In the insular construction industry, without repeat customers, you'll go out of business. Maintaining a consistently happy customer base puts WBCCs at the top of the list in project pursuit. The best measure of a customer's satisfaction is the award of the next project. However, if you wait until the next award is due to get that feedback, it'll be too late to impact the outcome of the award! Spending time proactively collecting customer satisfaction feedback through the course of your projects and trying to improve their experience along the way puts you more in control of your customers' satisfaction.

8. **Safety record.** While not obviously connected to net profit as a leading indicator, a company's safety record is important for reasons that rise far above profitability. WBCCs put the safety of their employees first because it's simply the right thing to do. Thankfully, industrywide, more owners are requiring their contractors to have a demonstrated positive safety record to be considered for their projects. This, along with rising insurance costs for poor performers, has created real business consequences for companies to focus on the safety of their employees. Often measured by checking a contractor's EMR (experience modification rating), there are now measurable ways to gauge a company's commitment to safety. This has drawn a clear connection between net profit and operating safely and raised the bar for all. Unsafe

companies won't be able to get the work they need to hit their revenue goals, and their net profits will fall apart.

Below is a sample of what a WBCC might do for measurement. It is not comprehensive but an illustration of this concept in action. Note the action-based leading indicators. These are the most critical items for companies following the principle of measuring what matters:

1. Determine a meaningful net profit target for the year.

2. Establish a budgeted overhead and stick to the budget monthly.

3. Determine how much gross profit is needed to cover overhead and leave you with your net profit target.

4. Based on a target gross profit percentage, determine the total revenue you must collect to achieve the total gross profit goal.

5. Monitor gross profit totals monthly and gross profit percentage on each individual project to ensure you're on track.

    □   Randomly review five estimates every month to check for accuracy, listing improvements for the team.

        »   Conduct estimating training in a monthly meeting to correct deficiencies.

    □   Complete a weekly audit of the project management software in a one-on-one with every project manager to ensure every job is on track with key milestones.

        »   Assess needs for coaching, training, and executive involvement.

        »   Conduct PM training in a monthly PM team meeting based on common challenges.

- Set daily progress goals for the field in a morning huddle for every project, and report on those goals using the field software at the end of each day.

  » Superintendent should work alongside each field employee for two hours, one on one, monthly to produce coaching and training opportunities to improve productivity.

6. Monitor total revenue monthly to ensure we're on track. Also, measure the leading indicators to total revenue monthly to ensure we're on pace for the future.

   - Maintain backlog projections of signed projects to spot any slowdowns with enough advance notice to adjust estimating behavior.

   - Maintain pipeline projections of potential projects to ensure we see enough new opportunities to fill our backlog needs for the future.

     » Conduct five customer meetings each month to talk about projects on the horizon.

     » Go to one industry networking event to meet new people and warm relationships.

7. Achieve a zero-safety incident year.

   - Conduct daily safety training on every jobsite each morning.

   - Conduct proactive weekly safety inspections of our own to spot and correct any issues.

   - Offer bonuses and incentives for outstanding safety performance.

As you determine how the concepts from this chapter fit in with your construction company, don't let it overwhelm you. Remember this rule: the data you gather is only as valuable as the action you take because of having it. With that in mind, don't feel like you must become a data-tracking machine like Google or Apple! Start with this simple question: What results am I less than satisfied with within my company? And follow that with this question: What issues are at the root of those unsatisfactory results? This will let you quickly isolate some action-based leading indicators that, if the right action is taken and we can prove it consistently, should lead to a better result.

One thing of great importance: for hitting your financial goals in business or at home, there is no substitute for having and sticking to a budget. Annually, WBCCs conduct a comprehensive budgeting process in which they establish earnings goals and spending limits for the business. Building and sticking to a budget can seem like a daunting task, but the power it provides as a tool for consistently steering the business to financial success is unparalleled.

Revenue and Resource Projections

We talked about the importance of the WIP in projecting the financial success of every project. This is an operational measure for active projects designed to inform management and staffing decisions. Revenue and resource projections across the company must also occur, and they're based on pipeline, sales, and backlog. Have you ever had a year when you did a ton of revenue and made less profit than much smaller revenue years? Yeah, that'll happen when you don't clearly see the wave coming and plan accordingly. Have you ever had a three-month dry spell right before a mountain of work begins that killed profits for the year because you had to hang onto all your billable staff to ensure you could produce when the big projects started? Yeah, that'll happen when you don't see the cliff in time and adjust your pricing and sales strategy to keep work coming in.

To produce these projections and reduce peaks and valleys, you should:

- Look at every project in your backlog and ask:

    □ When will this project start?

    □ How long will it run?

    □ What billable staff resources will be needed each month (or even week) as we look ahead?

- Look at every project in your pipeline and ask:

    □ What is the likelihood of us winning this project?

    □ When will this project start?

    □ How long will it run?

    □ What billable staff resources will be needed each month (or even week) as we look ahead?

- Take the monthly (or weekly) value and resource needs of each backlog project and spread the revenue across its duration.

- Take the monthly (or weekly) value and resource needs of each pipeline project adjusted down to the likelihood of winning it and spread the revenue across its duration. The combination of these things is a full revenue and resource projection.

- **Bonus round.** Include the projected gross profit for each project in your projections, and you'll also have the makings of a cash flow forecast!

How far out you run projections depends on your construction division, the markets you serve, and the size of projects you pursue. For some contractors, when you sell a project, you're close to staffing it and billing on it. Using the accrual system of accounting, which most contractors do, means you'll experience revenue right on the heels of a sale. In the tenant interiors market, for example, you rarely have a significant lag between the time you sell a project to the time you realize revenue from it. Tenant jobs are relatively small, and tenants want their space ASAP. Contractors in this environment don't have a significant backlog at any point, as projects run quickly. Perhaps you can see up to two or three months ahead in your backlog at a time. Resource and financial projecting for you are measured in single-digit months.

For other contractors, when you sell a project, you may not staff and begin billing for months. That means you sell something and put it in the backlog, delaying any revenue for quite some time. If you're building hospitals from the ground up—or stadiums, for example— you likely sell the project and have a long ramp-up period before you're up and billing on it. Some exceptions are some general contractors and the earliest-phase specialty contractors who are often expected to staff even megaprojects within weeks or days of getting a notice to proceed. This is owner driven and often due to permitting, funding, and other considerations, with owners working through issues before they can begin construction. However, even in these instances, the contractors often know with relative certainty that they're getting the project and have a sense of when it will start. WBCCs also know that start dates slide and adjust their projections, so if their client tells them they'll start in August, they project October because they have years of data to illustrate the average slippage of a projected start time by their client.

Whatever the circumstances, nailing revenue and resource projections is a core competency for WBCCs. They're never surprised about a ramp-up or slow-down, and their outstanding foresight lets them limit the peaks and valleys, making for a much smoother and more profitable operations experience.

CHAPTER 4

Master Meetings

Some contractors avoid meetings like the plague, and others are plagued by far too many. I've worked with clients who run the gamut, and there is a sweet spot. When you're gathering a group of your people for any amount of time, there must be a strong return on investment, and most contractors aren't getting enough of a return on their meetings, which is why many have stopped meeting entirely. Finding the right balance can be difficult and disheartening, but WBCCs have it down, and they thrive as a result. They're more efficient, better informed, and aligned behind a shared strategy. Here's how to master meetings.

Consistent Times and Agendas

There are meetings WBCCs view as essential to their business. We share the agendas for the three most important regular meetings for the foundation of a WBCC below. Consistency in times and agendas certainly applies to these most important of meetings, but they also apply to any recurring meetings you hold with your team.

Consistent time is so simple, yet so commonly the biggest issue with mastering meetings. Pulling multiple people together requires planning ahead, and when you let other things take precedence over your meeting times, causing you to constantly move them around, your meetings will be poorly attended and often canceled altogether. Pick a time and stick to it. Make it a time when you are highly unlikely to have a conflict. Clarify to all attendees that the meeting will not be moved to accommodate their schedule, which means they must move their schedule to accommodate the meeting. This is not too much to ask for a recurring meeting that everyone knows will happen on a specific time and date.

Having a consistent agenda enables attendees to learn how to effectively prepare, increasing the chances that the meeting is valuable. Your meeting should have an extremely clear objective. Build an agenda that cuts right to the heart of that objective, eliminate agenda items that distract from the meeting's core purpose, and distribute it with plenty of time for attendees to review and prepare. What are you meeting to accomplish? What is the best agenda to make that happen? Meetings should not aim to accomplish too many things. The preparation for an all-encompassing meeting is overwhelming and will lead to disappointment when people fail to meet the standard of preparation. It can be tempting to cover everything all at once, but long meetings with massive agendas are difficult to control. Save the marathons for annual retreats facilitated by professionals, not your regular recurring meetings.

Data-Driven

When meetings are not data driven, people show up to the meeting to discover what is happening. These are nightmare meetings for people who already know what is happening, as they must listen to people regurgitate information that could and should have been sent in a report via email. The purpose of the meeting should not be to discover what is happening but instead to discuss what to do about what is happening. This means people should review the relevant data before the meeting and prepare their questions and concerns for discussion in advance. Ideally, I'd even like those questions and concerns to be shared across the team in attendance prior to the meeting so people can think through their answers and reactions accordingly. Doing what I'm describing leads to wildly efficient meetings, in which we can cut to the core of the issues requiring discussion, derive meaningful action items, and get back to doing rather than talking.

Continuity between Meetings

If you've ever been in a weekly meeting, chances are you've experienced a lack of continuity. This is when we review the same things as last time as if we hadn't talked about them before. The primary culprit here is not having a shared document to capture meeting notes, particularly decisions and action items. The answer is to implement a tool to capture notes and action items that the whole team can view whenever they want. Some software has been developed specifically for this purpose. Products like Trello, Asana, and Bloom Growth come to mind. If you'd rather keep it simple, use a cloud-shared document in OneDrive or Google Docs. In addition to good documentation, the other key to continuity between meetings is beginning and ending meetings with an action item review. This brings a level of accountability and a sense of progress to the meeting. Repeat offenders who don't complete their action items must be held accountable for their lack of follow-through, or the bar will be lowered for the whole team.

I am a huge proponent of recording meetings as well. Many technologies today create searchable recordings and transcripts of your meetings that let you go to the points of most interest and review them. It eliminates "That's not what we agreed to" debates and proves extremely useful when you look at your list of action items and try to remember the spirit of it … just play back the recording.

Expectations for Contribution

When team members go to meetings and remain silent the entire time, it is a good bet they resent being there. If you aren't creating healthy interaction between all meeting attendees, just record the meeting and send it to the people you want to be informed but who don't need to contribute. Meetings are for dialogue, give-and-take, and problem-solving. Your recurring meetings should not be stumps for people to deliver one-hour speeches. This problem has become even more pervasive today in the time of the virtual meeting. Unlike in-person meetings, virtual meetings give cover to people who are blatantly multitasking while getting credit for their attendance. Attendees should not keep their laptops open so they can monitor email and work on other projects simultaneously. Companies that hold too many meetings allow this behavior because they feel guilty not allowing people to stay on top of things. Everyone must be totally present and engaged for meetings to be effective and efficient, so have fewer, better meetings.

Joining a highly interactive in-person or virtual meeting is a different experience. Each team member understands why they are there and what they're expected to contribute to the discussion. If they aren't expected to contribute, but you want them to be informed, send them the meeting recording or just the meeting notes afterward, and they can take five minutes to review what could have required an hour of their time at a specified time and place.

Clarity Meetings

The number and types of meetings you have will be unique to your construction business. Who needs to meet and how often depends a lot on your organizational structure. Ensure they conform to the rules about mastering meetings above, and do your best to keep them few and brief, but quality meetings are necessary. However, I've found there are just a few meetings that are universally necessary. These meetings are special because they provide a forum for unquestionably the most important conversations you will regularly have as a team. Without these meetings, people at every level in the business lack the crucial input to do their jobs at the highest possible level. I call these meetings "clarity meetings" because they clarify the path forward for all in attendance. Clarity meetings should focus and energize attendees toward a common course of action.

FINANCIAL CLARITY MEETING

The financial clarity meeting should happen monthly for a minimum of one hour. The conversation should focus first on the year-to-date profit-and-loss statement compared to the budget. The numbers should be viewed beforehand by all meeting participants in a summary format initially, looking at the broad categories of revenue, direct costs, and overhead.

Compare each figure to the budgets you established at the beginning of the year. When you're ahead or behind in each category, drill down into what's causing it, and let the discussion begin. Remember, we're following the rules on mastering meetings, so we've already reviewed the metrics before the meeting and have our reactions, questions, and concerns prepared for discussion. We're not meeting to find out how we're performing financially; we're meeting to discuss what is happening and determine action items to continue to press our advantage or fix something. For example, we are overspending on overhead related to software. The discussion leads to an action item to list all software users and conduct a study to determine whether we need all the licenses we're paying for. The meeting agenda is:

- Action item review from the previous meeting (five minutes)

- List the areas where we are ahead and behind (ten minutes)

- List and prioritize discussion topics based on the metrics (two minutes)

- Discuss each topic thoroughly to derive an action item (forty minutes)

  - Some issues may not be solved in the meeting. When this is identified, set an action item to hold a separate discussion about it later with the right people. Keep the meeting moving.

- Review action items from this meeting to confirm everything is captured (three minutes)

  - Who is responsible, and when is it due?

This meeting should be held between the owners or chief executive and the highest-level finance members of the team, whether that's a controller or CFO. Some owners are sensitive to expanding this group beyond that. However, I strongly recommend expanding the group to include leaders of operating groups. By that, I mean leaders with both top-line (sales) and bottom-line (operations) responsibility in any area of the business. You may hold a financial review for their metrics and leave them out of the broader company financials if you choose, but I would argue that transparency on the numbers to the executive team is a good and healthy thing for owners to embrace. If you, as an owner, are not comfortable with your executive team seeing how much money the business is earning, it is a sign of a lack of trust or sense of guilt.

If it's a lack of trust, go fix that. Having a trusted team of executives in the real trenches with you is a powerful thing, and it is a shame to waste that potential. Have the difficult conversations with your executives about why you don't trust them, and work on your relationship or replace them with people you do trust. However, sometimes you are the problem. You don't trust because of your own issues, not theirs. Get over that, or you'll feel the inevitable consequences of losing your top people because you never treat them like true executives.

For more on Mastering Meetings, make sure you
sign up for the Topping Out newsletter at
www.wellbuiltconsulting.com/toppingout.

If you're feeling guilty about showing your executive team how much the company makes, it is possible that you've got mental baggage about the issue. Making a lot of money is both idolized and demonized in our society. Everyone wants to make money, and we idolize those who have made their fortunes. But when we find out that our boss is making a lot of money, that idolatry can turn to resentment. Why is that? There is absolutely no shame in an owner reaping the lion's share of the benefit in return for their risk and investment. Your executive team will get that, and if they don't, you need to sit them down and help them to understand what it took for you to start the business. Let go of the mental baggage and stop feeling guilty—that is, unless you feel you should share more of the profits with the executive team.

Sharing the wealth with your executive team is not only a good idea but can also be a multiplier for your business. With the right structure, you can align them with the company's net profit goals completely, driving better results for the business and increasing their personal income. Every WBCC has a profit-sharing plan, whether they've brought employees into the ownership pool, converted to an employee stock ownership program (ESOP), or just created transparent bonus plans tied to gross profit or net profit. Being generous and open about company profitability builds trust and empathy with your team.

ESTIMATING CLARITY MEETING

The estimating function is the *get work* function for contractors. The focus of this clarity meeting is to ensure we're achieving the revenue budget. If you have multiple business units, such as a drywall division and masonry division or a Missouri office and an Arkansas office, there should be multiple estimating meetings. The meeting should happen weekly and include everyone involved in the estimating function and the executives responsible for the business unit. The meeting agenda should be as follows based on the rules of mastering meetings, so the appropriate information is fully reviewed in advance and discussion ensures in the meeting:

- Action item review from the last meeting (five minutes)

- Win/loss summary from the previous week (five minutes)

- Go/no-go review (ten minutes)

  □ Review the scorecards on potential opportunities, and use that data to determine whether each opportunity justifies pursuit. Document action items throughout. *We will cover this tool in more detail later.*

- Pipeline strategy (thirty-five minutes)

  □ Discuss the latest happenings with high-value target projects, and develop strategies to improve our likelihood of winning. Strategies range from adjusting pricing and suggesting VE options to leveraging relationships and planning business development events. Document action items throughout.

- Action-item review (five minutes)

Monthly, the estimating meeting should include an overall metrics review to ensure it is on track. These metrics are:

- Win rate

- Estimating pacing

- Sales pacing

Every contractor has a win rate, which is a formula of projects won v. projects lost over a rolling twelve-month period reflected as a percentage. For example, you won ten projects and lost thirty, so your win rate is 10/40 or 1 in 4 (25 percent). Do not include projects on which you remain in pursuit in this calculation, as you do not know the outcome on them yet. Based on your revenue goals and the target number of projects you need to achieve them, you should have an estimating pacing goal that reflects the amount you must estimate to win what you need. You set your estimating pacing requirements based on your win rate, so checking in on it monthly is important.

Staying with the 25 percent win rate, a company that needs to win $20 million must estimate $80 million, which translates to about $6 million per month. That $6 million per month is your estimating pacing goal. Likewise, your sales pacing goal is $1.67 million per month to achieve $20 million for the year. As you set your pacing goals, bear in mind that selling $20 million is different from having a $20 million revenue year. Refer to the prior section on revenue and resource projections for more on this. Selling $20 million this year, depending on the time between selling and building work, could mean anything from $20 million in revenue this year to $0 in revenue this year.

OPERATIONS CLARITY MEETINGS

Operations is the *build work* function in your business, and this team must be in lockstep with each other on the path forward on their projects. There are different operations clarity meetings to account for the many facets that go into building the work. There are:

- Handoff clarity meetings
- Kickoff clarity meetings
- Production clarity meetings
- Morning huddles

Estimating-to-PM Handoff Clarity Meeting

If the estimating function is performed by a different person from project management in your business, the first handoff clarity meeting is between estimating and project management. The PM must get the project set up administratively and begin processes ranging from budget development to preparing submittals and everything between. This meeting should happen within three weeks of being awarded the project and much faster if the start date is pressing. The meeting should be between the estimating staff who bid the project and the PM staff, including the head of the operations function in this business unit, project executives; PMs; assistant PMs; and project engineers. A thorough handoff clarity meeting between estimating and project management ranges from one to four hours or even longer, depending on the complexity of the project. Follow a checklist for the meeting covering every aspect of the project the PM team should know about before taking it over. Minimize storytelling and complaining in this meeting; you have a lot to cover. The meeting agenda is your handoff checklist, which should be unique to your business.

PM-to-Field Handoff Clarity Meeting

Some WBCCs, especially GCs, succeed at including field leadership in the handoff from estimating, which is good for efficiency. However, for most, a separate handoff clarity meeting from the PM to the field is necessary. This is due to the PM being responsible for building the project budget, selecting vendors and subs, and creating the first schedule and other items that the field must be briefed on, and that information is not available until the PM has the project. The PM-to-field handoff clarity meeting is to align the PM and field management staff on their approach to building the project, match resource and manpower plans to the schedule up front, and get a head start on solving any foreseeable challenges together. Attendees for this meeting are the PM team outlined above and the field team, beginning with the head of field operations for this business unit, the superintendents, assistant superintendents, field engineers, and forepersons who will work on this project. The meeting should take place no more than two weeks before the project is set to kick off and up to four weeks if time allows. The same as the estimating handoff clarity meeting, this meeting should be one to four hours and longer if needed, be run using a checklist, and kept strictly on the agenda to get through everything. The meeting agenda is your handoff checklist, which should be unique to your business.

Kickoff Clarity Meetings

Once your PM and field teams have ownership of the project, you're ready for a kickoff clarity meeting with the client. Some of your clients may hold these meetings already, which is great because you don't have to convince them to meet, but it also means you must ensure your agenda is covered as well as theirs. The purpose of this meeting is expectation setting. You're confirming your scope and identifying clear lines of communication for each type of discussion; for example: Whom do we talk to about change orders? RFIs? You are also sharing what you need from one another to be successful on the project, as well as what is unacceptable. This is also a good time to ask in advance for help you know you might need or share concerns you have about things like materials availability or on-site logistics. The meeting should include all PM and field staff from your team as well as the field and the related staff from your client. For a specialty contractor, this meeting should be one to two hours with your GC client. For a GC, this meeting spans a full day with your owner client and ideally would include the architect. I am often asked by GCs to facilitate this meeting and use it as a forum to create teamwork from the start. The agenda, if you can dictate it, should be:

- Thorough scope review

- Schedule and phasing review

- Safety program review

- Mutual expectations

- Action-item review

PRODUCTION CLARITY MEETINGS

This meeting should occur weekly for no more than two hours to ensure every project has a strong plan for success in the weeks ahead. The attendees are the PM staff and higher-level field leadership staff for all projects for this business unit. I recommend that projects become a part of the operations clarity meeting two weeks before their scheduled start date, letting the team begin talking about them as a team before they get underway. A good production clarity meeting should be mostly reaffirming the plan on every project and checking alignment with some opportunity for coaching and problem-solving by leaders in the room. This is a good chance to help one another by sharing with colleagues what has worked in similar situations. There's also a measure of accountability in this meeting created by each project team stating their goals for the week ahead and reporting on progress from the prior week. The agenda is:

- Action-item review from last week's meeting (ten minutes)

- Project-by-project presentation of status by the PM or super on that project (thirty to sixty) minutes

  - Did you accomplish last week's goals?

    » If not, why not, and how can the group help?

- What are this week's goals?

  - Group offers suggestions for meeting this week's goals.

  - Goals and action items for the week ahead are captured and assigned to individuals

- Coaching by the leadership team (up to thirty minutes)

- Review all action items to ensure nothing was missed (five minutes)

MORNING HUDDLES

No other form of clarity meeting has ever made a bigger positive impact on my clients over the years than the morning huddle. This simple, fifteen-minute meeting prevents more problems and creates more teamwork than you can imagine. The premise is simple. Pull together the teams working together at the beginning of each day to review the day before, set goals for the day, and spot needs for support. Knowing the huddle is coming each day lets people keep notes on the things they need from one another rather than constantly interrupting during a busy workday. The huddle creates a sense of being in the trenches together and being accountable to your fellow team members. There's magic in it if you put it in place. The meeting time should be capped at fifteen minutes, and any additional conversation can be planned to occur after. The agenda is:

- Each person presents (one to five minutes each)

  □ Their performance versus goal from the day before

  □ Their goals for today

  □ What support or advice they need from anyone else in the meeting

- Review the list of things people need from one another (one minute)

Summary of the Foundation

Again, I would not recommend implementing anything else you read in this book before implementing every aspect of the Foundation. It doesn't matter if your business has a great five-year plan or an amazing marketing strategy; if you don't own the fundamentals of becoming a WBCC, you will not unleash your full potential. If you don't achieve financial transparency, you'll never be confident about your business's health or know what is necessary to right the ship. You will underperform your net profit goals, and when, by luck, you succeed, it will be fleeting and impossible to replicate. If you don't measure what matters, you'll struggle to control your profit outcomes, as you place your focus only on lagging rather than leading indicators. You will be frustrated with your management team, but they can't manage things that have already happened. If you don't master meetings, you will either waste valuable resources in low-value meetings, or you'll avoid them altogether. In either case, the team will be out of alignment and operating in isolated silos.

However, with the Foundation in place, you can confidently build the construction company of your dreams. With financial confidence, control over the metrics that matter, and a strong set of communication habits, your team can handle anything together.

Engineering a Clear Strategic Direction

When faced with opportunities and challenges, businesses and, indeed, all people must be able to rely on some established decision-making system to know what is right and wrong for them. We all have those systems, whether we realize it or not. Our decision-making systems are a combination of our brains' innate wiring and the norms with which we were raised through our families and society. Many construction companies lack decision-making systems for their organizations, leaving critical decisions about how to handle opportunities and challenges to the individual decision-making of their employees. While this can work out just fine, it sure leaves a lot to chance. Construction companies without organizational guidance for critical decisions often have too many irons in the fire and a lack of focus on a shared set of priorities. They struggle to hire for critical positions or replace people when they leave. They take on projects that aren't good fits for the company. They open branches in new locations, only to close them a few years later when the work dries up. They keep the wrong employees and lose the ones they should keep, and so on.

WBCCs have a system for decision-making that lets their people confidently pursue or disregard new opportunities and initiatives and overcome their challenges in a way that aligns with their goals. This system derives from the clear strategic direction (CSD) the company puts in place. To be clear, great companies are still made up of intelligent, talented individuals who maintain agency over the daily decisions they must make to perform their roles. Individual thinking and creativity are crucial to success in the modern business environment. The CSD discussed in this chapter must not prevent you from building a team of capable people with solid decision-making skills. Instead, a CSD should implant a set of additional factors to consider when evaluating a course of action in the face of challenges and opportunities in the minds of those talented people.

CSD comes from enacting these steps:

1. Gain owner clarity.

2. Choose a brand identity.

3. Build and follow a strategic business plan.

4. Review progress on the strategic plan.

5. Update the strategic plan.

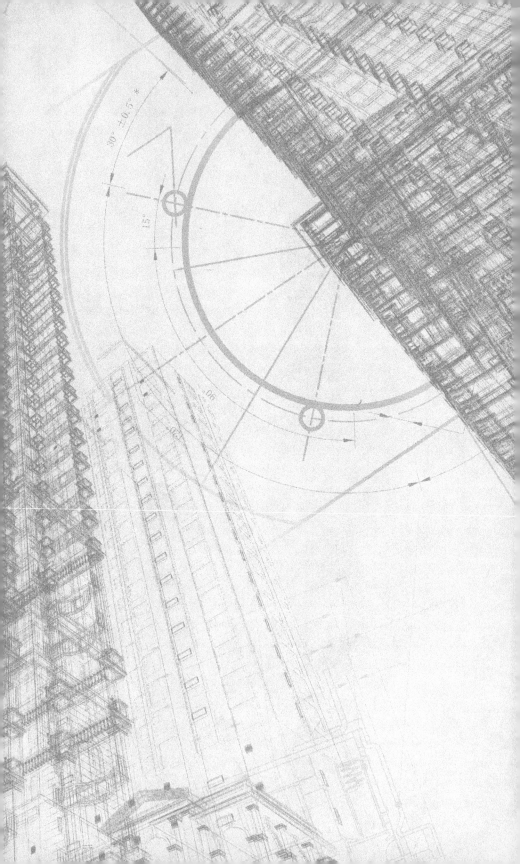

CHAPTER 5

Gain Owner Clarity

Whatever the ownership structure, the CSD of a business must align with the goals of the owner or owners. The business owner is the source of funding for the company. They decide how much income to take from the business and approve operating budgets, putting them at the center of any decision they wish to make. Construction companies in which the owners are not supportive of the company's direction are doomed to feel like they're battling for funding to pursue any of their initiatives. If the owner doesn't understand or value what the executives are trying to accomplish, why would they write a check? Feeling pressured, I've seen situations where executives force their owners to fund company initiatives. This unwanted pressure can put the owner in the strange circumstance of emotionally rooting for their investment to fail. How dysfunctional is that?

One time a company's executive team hired me, much to the owner's dismay, to help them develop a three-year strategic plan for the business. The owner skipped important preparation meetings and avoided my calls and emails, and in the rare moments he was present for our discussions, he was actively disengaged, working on his computer instead. His actions told me he was not on board with the effort, but I wasn't sure why. After reaching the halfway point in our preretreat preparation, I confronted him directly, asking what was wrong. He described how he didn't see the value in developing a strategic plan for the business. In his view, informed by thirty-plus years at the helm of this business, the construction industry was wholly unpredictable. Any attempts to build a plan would inevitably fail due to surprises.

The younger generation of leadership, however, had a very different view of the future. Once we identified this disconnect between the owner and his executive team, I brought it to a group discussion. I moderated it so they could decide whether a strategic plan even made sense in their business. Feeling heard for the first time, the owner shared his position that planning was pointless. Saying it aloud in front of the group made his position on planning sound silly! Of course, a company can't plan for everything, but floating along without a plan was a recipe for disaster, and everyone saw it. The owner laughed at himself as he was talking and finally shared that the real reason for his apathy toward the plan was his own lack of desire to take the company to the next level. He was tired, and the only plan he was interested in had him sitting on a beach in five years. The team could get on board with enabling the owner to live that vision! A unifying idea in their strategic plan was creating a clear path for the owner to move on, which got the owner excited in the planning process and pulled the team together. Without this alignment, the plan would have been toothless without the owner's support, and it would have likely led to the frustrated departure of key members of his executive team.

Owners can prevent disconnects from damaging their companies by clarifying what matters most to them personally. As a business owner, knowing what you want your life to look like means determining how the business must look. There are many books about personal goal-setting and schools of thought for building a personal vision. Therefore, I will keep my advice on personal goal-setting succinct and encourage those with deeper questions to explore other resources of which this subject is the sole topic.

Personal Goal-Setting

People need goals in all areas of life to be well rounded. While everyone's needs are nuanced, we all share seven areas for personal goals. Those areas include relationships, health and wellness, personal growth, life experiences, career achievements, contribution, and material things. When we fail to focus on any of the seven areas that are most important to us, we sense a lack of balance in our lives. For example, many business owners and executives focus on career achievement and the resulting material things that come with the money they make, only to reach a point in their life when they realize they haven't focused enough on their health or relationships. Being sick and alone with their money and material things was not what they would have planned for themselves, yet there they are. Had they been more intentional about their personal goals sooner, they may have hired successors and reduced their involvement in their businesses so they could spend more time with loved ones and exercise more regularly. I use this stereotypical example for its simplicity in driving home the point that for business owners, the choices they make about how they want to live their lives will directly affect the decisions they make about structuring the business. A lack of personal clarity will result in becoming unhappy with the business in the long run.

If you haven't set out your goals in writing, start there. Using the list of the seven areas above for inspiration, document your goals. Goals should be specific so you can measure their attainment. *Exercise five days each week* is a better goal than *get into shape*. Goals should stretch the boundaries of your mental limitations while remaining something you believe you can reach. Nobody is allowed to decide what you are capable of but you, so take the chains off and dream a little. Once you have your goals written down, share them with loved ones and work on building them together. After loved ones, share your goals with mentors. People who know what you're trying to achieve will seek ways to help you through advice, opportunities, and accountability. Consider creating a visual representation of your goals you can look at each day on your wall or computer screen. Revise your goals every year with your loved ones and sometimes more often, depending on major life events. These steps will help you keep in touch with your motivations and help to guide decision-making in the business that aligns with what matters to you personally. I would recommend the process above to every reader, but the exercise takes on more significance for the business owner for the reasons I've outlined above.

Consider the checklist below when thinking about personal goals that directly affect the business:

- How much money do you want to have from the business?

  - From income and distributions annually

  - From your eventual exit

- When, if ever, do you want to walk away from the business?

- Is it important to you that the business continues to operate after you walk away?

- Do you want to keep ownership in the family?

- Is there someone you want to succeed you?

- In your remaining working years, what do you want your role to be in the business?

  □ What are you best at?

  □ What do you enjoy most?

  □ What do you enjoy least you know you don't want to do anymore?

Build your Role to Match Your Personal Vision

The owner of a two-hundred-employee specialty contractor found his job stressful and unsatisfying. He loved the technical side of his business and particularly enjoyed preconstruction efforts. The business was initially built on the value general contractors and owners placed on his ability to recognize opportunities to close scope gaps and create value-engineering solutions. He was a genius in this capacity, leading to rapid growth to two hundred employees in just under five years. At some point in the journey, he realized he couldn't keep up with it all and hired a director of preconstruction so he could focus on running the business. This was when the stress and unhappiness began. Everything changed for the better one day when he realized that the company's owner didn't need to run the company. With this idea in mind, he began the search for a president and found an incredible candidate. Within a year, the new president had the business running like a top, and the owner went back to lead the preconstruction effort for the business.

With the owner happier than ever in his role, the combination of a stellar president and an unmatched preconstruction department cemented their position in the market, and their business easily grows today.

Whatever thought made this owner believe he had to be the one running the company was wrong, and he had proven it. How many owners are playing roles in their businesses that they're genuinely not suited for? When this happens, it hurts both the owner and the company. It takes a humble owner to recognize their role may not be active in leadership, but if more owners made this determination, they and their companies would be happier for it. In the scenario I described above, the owner retained authority over the company's strategic direction and full ownership at the time of this writing. He didn't remove himself from many key business decisions. He simply recognized his limitations in management and listened to his heart about what role the business needed him to play and where he would be happiest, then structured the business to match his personal goals.

As the owner, you should be aware of the tendency for owners to play roles that are totally indispensable to the company. I've known many owners who find themselves at a loss when they're ready to exit the business because they're far too integral to the daily operation. If you ever want to exit, you must ensure the business can run perfectly well without your involvement. There are phases of business, the same as there are phases to life. Early on, it makes sense for the owner to be deeply involved in building the business. There's very limited room to add management overhead, so the owner is often the CEO, president, and VP of operations or estimating. That's appropriate for a small contracting company in its early stages. If the company wishes to graduate from that phase and scale up, the owner must give up some of their roles. In this next phase, the owner should reduce their involvement to only one or two roles.

While that is often CEO and president, as shown by the story above, it doesn't have to be. I've found the best role for owners who plan to exit at some point is chairperson of the board or CEO. This lets them guide the strategic direction of the business and help wherever necessary but removes them from daily decision-making, as that is handled by the president and various departmental heads. But VP of preconstruction is also perfectly acceptable for an exiting owner if there's a clear successor ready to step into that position.

Gaining owner clarity remains relevant if your construction company has an ownership *team* today rather than a single owner. However, as you might imagine, it takes on another layer of complexity. With multiple owners, it becomes even more important to gain owner clarity before building a strategic business plan. I've seen misaligned owners create an incredible number of problems for their companies. At the center of all their business problems are significant differences in opinion between the owners playing out publicly. Having two or more people maintain a shared vision over a long period of time is possible, but it requires excellence in communication, combined with cooperation and a willingness to compromise. This is the goal, but it is not possible for everyone. I strongly recommend always having a majority owner, even with only 1 percent more equity, to ensure the company's ability to take decisive action despite disagreements between the ownership. This, along with an operating agreement that clearly spells out how owners may sell their stakes at any time, allows companies with multiple owners to build strategic business plans for the good of the organization, even if there's trouble between the owners. The worst thing that happens in this case is that irreconcilable differences cause a split in the ownership, but the company continues forward.

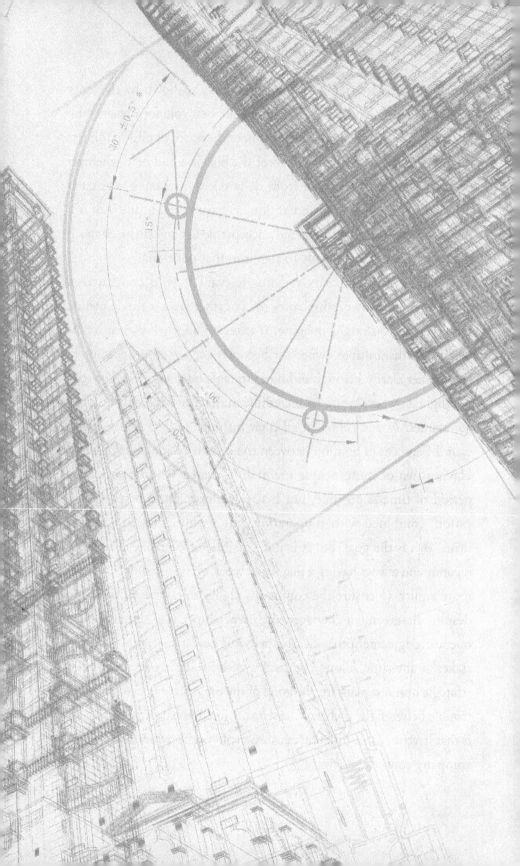

CHAPTER 6

Build a Strategic Business Plan

Pause and reflect on where your company is today, the type and number of employees you have, the customers you serve, the types of work you're doing, etc. How much of where you are right now would you say was all part of the plan versus opportunistic or even random? In my experience, there will always be a mixture of the planned and the random. It is impossible to plan for every contingency. For the best strategic planners in the building industry, if their mix of planned versus random is better than 50 percent, they consider it a win. Because so much in this industry can feel out of your control, there is a constant temptation to leave the whole thing to chance and just try your best every day. There is something appealing and even valid in that thought. Letting go of trying to control things that are out of your control and just keeping your head down and doing your best is wise advice on some level. People who try to assert their control over every little thing will find themselves constantly overrun by glitches that couldn't be planned for, in a constant state of stress and frustration, and often so obsessed with the illusion of control over their lives and businesses they miss the bigger picture and run things into the ground. Still, although it's futile to plan for everything, it is downright irresponsible to plan for nothing, isn't it? The family who builds their house in a flood zone without trying to grade the property for ideal drainage and build on a deep-pier foundation is begging for disaster. They're not just letting go of the things outside of their control; they are also failing to control the steps that might protect them in the face of likely adverse events. Sure, they can't control how high the water might rise or the ferocity with which the current rips away at their land and foundation, but they can research both and build accordingly.

The secret of WBCCs is that they seek to control the controllable. They set the course of their businesses firmly in the direction they want, assess the actions necessary to evolve into that type of business, and take deliberate action toward their desired direction. Meanwhile, they are always trying to face and educate themselves about as many of the potential problems and opportunities they might face, so they can make their companies more resistant, resilient, and nimble when they encounter those problems and opportunities. Not all uncontrollables are bad! You have as little control over a booming construction market as you do over a recessionary one. Your planning should consider both opportunities and threats. This combination of building toward an ideal version of themselves and confronting the difficult realities they may face along the way is central to what lets WBCCs outperform 98 percent of their peer companies. Everything you will learn after this chapter flows from your commitment to building and following your strategic business plan. You must seek to control that which is controllable and be at peace with that which you cannot control.

Building a documented strategic business plan can seem like a daunting task. You and your team are likely too focused on the daily grind of putting quality work in place safely and efficiently to think much about who you want to be when you grow up. As Michael Gerber coined it in his book *The E-Myth*, you are likely too busy working *in* your business to work *on* it.[1] Strategic business planning is very much working on the business, and the importance of stepping back from the day-to-day and asking the big questions that will determine the future of your business cannot be overstated. Still, there are more urgent things happening in every construction company's world today that make it challenging to justify taking the time to disconnect from preconstruction, operations, production, accounting, and HR to build and make progress on your strategic plan. In this section, I will simplify building a strategic plan so you can put real-time expectations on the exercise for your company. There are six steps to strategic planning:

1. Goal-setting

2. Articulation of core values (simple rules)

3. Discovery

4. Retreat planning

5. Departmental Initiatives

6. Plan documentation and communication

---

1   Michael E. Gerber, *The E-Myth: Why Most Businesses Don't Work and What to Do about It* (New York: HarperCollins, 2012).

Goal-Setting

Where do you want to find yourself in business three years from now? What will be different and better than it is today? Your goals are allowed to be whatever you want. Nobody gets to decide whether your goals are too big or too small. I'll share some simple guidelines for goal-setting here, but as with everything in this book, these are mere guidelines. I've seen too many ways of setting goals that work for businesses to say there is one definitive way. It starts with your mindset.

BELIEVE IN YOUR GOALS

If you're going to be the type of company that meets the goals you've set, you must internalize a company identity that supports the kind of thought and action needed. In his book *What to Say When You Talk to Your Self*, Shad Helmstetter makes a compelling case that the human mind is like a computer, and the thoughts we have about ourselves are like the software programs we're running on our computers.[2] What you tell yourself repeatedly, you will tend to make a reality. That's not mystical; it's the clear connection between our thoughts and actions. What we think is true will influence our actions, and our actions have results. Those results will reaffirm our beliefs since we acted in alignment with our current beliefs. This equally applies to companies as it does to individuals. If our executive team walks around thinking, "We're no different or better than our competition," we won't be investing in improvement. We've told our brains not to think that way!

I know this is a little touchy-feely, but before the company can embrace planning and acting on its goals, it must collectively redefine

---

2   Shad Helmstetter, *What to Say When You Talk to Your Self* (New York, NY: Gallery Books, 2017).

its identity by telling itself who it is and who it will become. As an individual and company, your past will dictate your future only if you fail to redefine yourself. In my time consulting with over one hundred construction companies, I have noticed the biggest obstacle to achieving bold, new goals is the inertia caused by a lack of belief that they can be achieved. Securing that belief starts at the top and requires repetition.

Here's the action step: simply ask yourself, "If this company had already achieved these compelling goals, what would we be saying about ourselves?" The answers to that question should become the way you describe yourselves internally. Your team should talk about itself in glowing terms among one another! Examples of this in action might be:

- "We are the clear choice for podium structures in northern Alabama."

- "Our commitment to employee development makes us widely recognized as one of the best places to work in Houston."

- "We are opening a third location in two years."

- "Our executive team is growing. That means lots of opportunities for advancement."

- "We are developing fabrication capabilities that will improve efficiency and value for our clients."

One general contracting firm built a strong business focusing on one specific market segment over the years. They built millions of square feet in that sector over a few decades and were well known in the community for this work. Looking at the market trends and the future of that sector, they wanted to diversify their work into other market sectors. In the early days after making that strategic goal of diversification, they struggled to reimagine their possibilities outside what they had always done. "We know how to build in one sector ..." the team would say, and it would crush strategic diversification ideas before they ever got going. One day they realized that nobody was allowed to decide their identity but them and that they could choose who they wanted to become. This changed things entirely.

Instead of getting stuck on how they had always defined themselves, they embraced a new internal definition of themselves. They didn't turn their backs on their roots but instead embraced that segment as a part of what they do exceptionally well and simply added the new market segments they were committed to pursuing to that list. "We serve three segments ..." became their new mantra. "We're well diversified and have teams specializing in those three areas." At first, it was more aspirational than factual, but that proclamation became true over a five-year timeline. At the time of this writing, about five years later, the business is split between about 40/40/20, with their original sector making up one of the 40 percent categories. They've more than doubled in size over that timeframe and taken significant market share from the competition in the other sectors while maintaining and even slightly growing their core sector market share.

It was a lot of work for this company to manifest its goals into reality. I don't want to minimize the investment of time, money, and energy to make this happen. Still, I want to underscore that no action could have been taken if the company didn't embrace its new identity. The turning point for this company was when the team saw itself differently. That led to discussions about their believable diversification strategy, not just pipe dreams. Those believable discussions turned into action plans being carried out, and the rest is history.

The company I referenced in this story aimed to diversify into distinct markets. That kind of choice isn't for everyone. For them, it meant massive overhauls to their internal processes, a hiring strategy to attract talent from competitors in the market sectors they wished to pursue, and a costly, time-intensive marketing and business development push. It was expensive and disruptive, but it worked.

THREE ELEMENTS OF BUSINESS GOALS

First, the achievement of the goal must matter. Accomplishing the goal must attach to something deep and emotional for the executive team and, ideally, for everyone in the company. Let's imagine, like our example company above, you had a goal of diversifying the markets you serve. What is driving that goal? Perhaps market diversification is related to a deep desire for self-determination and preservation. You refuse to ignore the signs of a changing market and do nothing to adapt and thrive. Diversification in that context means keeping your great employees and keeping food on the table of the families for those hardworking employees. It also means refusing to be a victim of the market and being overtaken by the inevitable shrinking of your core market. The goal of diversification is actually about pride, ingenuity, and survival. The reason a goal must matter is simple: it will be a pain in the ass to make the goal a reality, and everyone better be all-in, or you'll come up with excuses not to make it happen. Do your goals for your business matter at an emotional and even a primal level? If not, get back to work on them and find the fire that will fuel you and your team to do hard things.

Just an aside here: You may not need to change your goals if your answer was no to the question about goals mattering emotionally. You may just need to dig into your deeper personal motivations for meeting your goals and tap into why you set that goal in the first place. I have a goal of flossing my teeth every day, which doesn't seem all that emotional and primal to me when I think about it, but underneath the surface, I'm terrified of the pain of losing my teeth, undergoing root canals, etc. In other words, if you explore most of your goals, you'll find an emotional desire fueling them somewhere. If you explore the desire and it's just not there, however, move on and improve your goals.

Second, your goals should be specific and vivid. Sticking with the diversification example, you'd set out a three-year diversification plan showing the target revenue growth and diversity in revenue for each year of that plan. You wouldn't let your goal be a vague nod to improve diversification. You would call out the clients you'll have in each new market sector and the size and type of projects you'll perform. Setting your course with such specificity and detail brings your goals to life. Many books have been written on why and how this works. Some that I'd recommend you read, like Napoleon Hill's *Think and Grow Rich* and Cameron Herold's *Vivid Vision*, will get deep into the psychology and prove this methodology works and is worthwhile. If you're like me, however, and you're looking for practical application more than theory, just take my word for it … this is legit. Companies that decide where they want to go and build momentum behind a vision are considerably more likely to achieve uncommon success. So are your goals detailed, specific, and vivid? In addition to asking yourself that question, you might also ask people in your life whom you can trust to be candid.

Third, your goals should align appropriately with the market. If the market has no interest in or need for the kind of company you wish to become, your goals will never manifest into a thriving business concept. Before setting your goals, complete a market analysis and speak with your employees, customers, and allies in the market to gauge the market's interest in what you're thinking. Using the diversification example, you would use all available market trend data, along with interviews with your customers about the future of their market sectors, to determine the need for improved diversification. You would also participate in many industry trends meetings and conferences to get your finger on the pulse of where the market was heading before selecting your new target markets. The bottom line is just to make sure you are pursuing a future that has promise before investing your energy and resources.

Articulation of Core Values (Simple Rules)

In their effort to reach their goals, companies necessarily begin to act differently than they have in the past. If you want different results, you must take different action, right? However, too often, companies succeed in reaching the financial outcomes they want at the cost of losing their culture somewhere along the way. Having clearly articulated core values can prevent that culture erosion by cementing what you love about who you are as a company when you are at your best into guidelines for decision-making at every level in the business. WBCCs don't have a list of meaningless platitudes representing their core values listed in their company handbook; they use their core values to run their business. To bring them to life, WBCCs translate their core values into "simple rules" for that reason.

In their book *Simple Rules: How to Thrive in a Complex World*, Kathleen M. Eisenhardt and Donald Sull describe the value of having clear guidelines for decision-making[3]. The idea behind simple rules is to provide easy-to-retain guidelines, increasing the likelihood of decisions in line with what matters most. Simple rules provide flexibil-

---

3   Donald Sull and Kathleen M. Eisenhardt, *Simple Rules: How to Thrive in a Complex World* (Boston, MA: Mariner Books, 2016).

ity, where your documented business processes are more prescriptive. With this flexibility, people can be efficient with decision-making with the confidence they'll be at least directionally correct. One quote from the book summarizes their importance nicely: "Simple rules minimize the risk of overweighing peripheral considerations by focusing on the criteria most crucial for making good decisions."[4] Core values help you create the essential simple rules for your business. These criteria for making good decisions will prevent you and your team from choosing actions that erode your culture. Having a value of integrity is nice, but what's the related guidance you want people to consider when making decisions? It would be best to have the simple rule read: "Integrity: Always do the ethical thing, even when it is difficult, costs us money, or makes us look bad. You'll always look worse when caught in a lie."

Simple rules like these are teachable, are able to be retained, and can be gauged in action in every team member. I recommend capping simple rules at eight. Too many more become impossible to recall easily. When developing this list, consider who you are, but also consider who you want to become as an organization. Select the values you want to embody most, not just the ones you embody today. If they're already one and the same, you have a phenomenal culture. Note that it's nearly impossible to find a core value you don't like. Integrity, hard work, commitment, respect … I mean, who wouldn't want to be all these things? The trick is to identify the eight or fewer that are most important to your company's DNA.

One company, a sixty-employee MEP contractor, put service as their number-one value.

Their simple rule for service read: "Service: We believe in creating unparalleled service experiences for our employees and customers.

---

4   Ibid, p.36.

Nothing is more important than the service we provide, certainly not profit."

This is a successful midsize contractor that makes a nice profit, which was an important business outcome for them, but it did not come before service … nothing did. When a new employee made the decision to void an invoice to an unhappy client and send a crew back out to get the project corrected within twenty-four hours, she was admittedly nervous but confident in the choice. The owner recognized her commitment to service in their monthly newsletter and shared the story as a perfect example of the core values at work. You might disagree completely with their approach, but you can't argue that the simple rule was operating there as intended by reinforcing the core value of service.

See the values our company has created at
https://www.wellbuiltconsulting.com/

What are your company's core values? If you don't know where to start, begin by paying attention to the things that make you feel most proud of your team. What value was behind that feeling of pride? Then think about the things that anger you most when you see them in action. What value was violated that caused your blood pressure to rise? List all of them. It might be a list thirty values long! Then force-rank them from most important to least important to you.

Personally, I like running this exercise with leadership teams so that they each must bring a list of their top ten most important values to the retreat, and we keep the shared top five to eight. Nailing down your core values and doing a great job communicating the associated simple rules throughout the company can have a positive effect on your culture immediately and will protect your culture from decisions that lead you astray in the pursuit of your vision.

Discovery

Imagine if you walked in from outside your organization for the first time today and you met with the owner to learn about the company's identity and its goals. Imagine next that you're asked to help get the business on track to meeting its goals. Looking at your business through fresh eyes enables you to see issues and opportunities you've been missing when you're working in the business from day to day. The things you take for granted, the good and the bad, would jump off the page to you as strengths and weaknesses. You'd have to slow down and listen to your employees and customers to learn the perspectives of the most important relationships inside and outside the company. You would need to do a deep dive into the financial reporting to make sense of the numbers and see the patterns that emerge and the potential explanations behind them. It is hard to do but is a valuable experience. Many organizations hire outside consultants to conduct the discovery process and provide a fresh take on the business. In fact, this is the starting point for every consulting engagement our firm has, and here I'll share the concepts we use to do it.

The discovery process begins with an internal assessment. Credible team members or consultants should explore key performance metrics to identify potential root causes of positives and negatives. The numbers are telling the story, so slow down and listen closely to them. The performance metrics review will lead you to a series of hypotheses you can explore in the discovery process. For example, let's assume the metrics say it's taking you 15 percent longer to finish projects than you first planned. Based on some clues, your hypothesis may be that project managers aren't actively managing and communicating about project schedules. You'll explore that hypothesis in the discovery process. Surveys, interviews, and observations of the employees are a great way to get a feel for your culture and employee engagement and to explore your hypotheses. Your team often knows what is wrong with the business. Getting them to open up about it can be challenging, so it is crucial to approach this process by setting the right tone that this is their opportunity to help shape the future of the business by highlighting our areas for improvement. Due to employees' hesitance to be totally candid with their bosses, you will usually receive more accurate results by hiring an outside party to conduct the discovery process. As a result of the internal assessment step, leaders should have a comprehensive picture of how the business sees its own strengths and weaknesses.

After looking inside the business, the discovery process should focus on the environment outside the business. Start with a survey-and-interview process with customers that will help you understand what matters most to them and how you stack up against the competition. Pull benchmarking data from around the industry to assess how your company compares to others in your business. Research economic trends that may affect your current markets or lead you to consider others. You'll learn some concerning things that cause you to want to protect the business from outside threats, and you'll learn about some exciting things that cause you to want to exploit opportunities in the market. Many internal and external discovery elements can be routinized annually, making regular strategic plan development and reviews a less daunting task. Through the external assessment, you should have a comprehensive picture of where the company fits into the market today and what threats and opportunities exist.

The discovery process should culminate with findings from every area of the business reflecting the strengths, weaknesses, opportunities, and threats (SWOT) you discovered. These findings become a tool you will use in a planning retreat to help with well-informed discussion and decision-making. With the goals you set for the company, the SWOT will help to surface the most important strategic initiatives for the team to pursue.

Retreat Planning

Select the team to participate in the planning retreat. You'll be reviewing the most intimate details of the business, and you don't want anyone holding back because of who is in attendance. Be sure the team you select for the retreat is the team you'd go to war with any day of the week. High trust and great communication are a must. It is also best if the team has a good diversity of opinions so there's valuable debate and you can avoid groupthink. Selecting this team can be more challenging than it seems. You want to strike the balance described above—the team you trust with the most intimate company information, and simultaneously a group representing diversity of thought. It's possible that to do this, you need to take an intermediate team-building step before heading to a retreat so you can build trust with your team.

There are many useful approaches to team building. Some of my favorites revolve around the use of personality testing tools such as DiSC and leadership development concepts like the Five Behaviors of a Team. This is another thing best accomplished with professional facilitation. Get everyone in the same room, and set the ground rules—tell them a successful team retreat will include candid discussions and hard feedback, and they all need to be comfortable with that. If someone can't handle that vulnerability, they are probably not the right person for the retreat. My perfect number of attendees is eight, give or take a couple. Much larger, and it is difficult for everyone to have a voice. And much smaller means we're missing important opinions from leaders who will be responsible for carrying out the plan. Ideally, the team would comprise ownership, other executive leadership, and departmental managers. Imagine the CEO and majority owner joined by their CFO or controller, president, operations leadership, estimating leadership, field operations leadership, human resources leadership, and business development leadership.

With the right team selected, go off-site, stay overnight at the same property, find some time during the retreat to have nonbusiness fun together as a team, and allow twelve to sixteen hours of meeting time over two days. The meeting agenda should be something like this:

1. **Retreat goals and expectations.** To ensure everyone is engaged in a long meeting environment like this, there should be no emails, texts, or calls interrupting the meeting. People should leave their devices (including laptops) closed unless they're opening them to take a specific note or add value to the meeting. The goal of your retreat will be some variation on "to create alignment behind a strategic plan that helps us achieve our goals."

2. **Planning horizon.** How far out are you looking with this plan? If you are struggling and in need of more immediate solutions to nagging problems, you may be building a highly detailed one-year recovery plan to right the ship. If you have a mature business with consistently positive results, you may be thinking about more long-term opportunities and threats,

so you'll build a five-year plan. We usually split that difference and build three-year plans with our clients but will flex
up or down depending on the circumstances.

3. **Team-building exercise to get the conversation flowing.**
There are a million icebreakers. Google them and select
something that fits your team. The goal is to get people comfortable talking and get personal to create an open environment to set a positive tone for the meeting.

4. **Review your goals and core values.** If you haven't established these, the retreat is a great place to build them. The
owners should come to the conversation with a vision for
the outcomes they want to create and the driving inspiration behind that vision, and their draft of the core values
statements prepared. Ideally, the team would have done the
same. When the team contributes to building the goals and
values, it elevates their personal buy-in to the direction of
the business.

5. **SWOT presentation and open discussion.** This is where
you review the findings from the discovery step. Allow plenty
of time for this step since the depth of your findings should
lead to extremely valuable discussion. What strengths do you
have, and how can you leverage them further? What weaknesses do you have, and how can you either work on them
or reduce any problems caused by them? What opportunities might the market hold that you can capitalize on, and
what can we do about them? And what threats might the
market hold that you must protect against, and what can we
do about them? When overlaid against your goals, which of

these strengths, weaknesses, opportunities, and threats are the most important to focus on for your success?

6. **Strategic initiative development.** An initiative is a commitment a company makes to improve itself. An initiative is strategic because it was selected above other potential initiatives for its relevance to helping the company achieve specific goals in the strategic plan. The answers to the SWOT questions listed above are the basis for these initiatives. For example, in the SWOT discussion, you may have identified a growing client as an opportunity and suggested you invest in that relationship further. There's your potential initiative. This step of the retreat reviews the potential initiatives from the SWOT discussion and prioritizes the top ones to pursue. Other ideas for initiatives may arise as you review and prioritize. Many ideas will not be pursued, so prepare the team for that. I usually recommend no more than three to five initiatives per department per year. Even that can be too much when a single person is involved in more than one department.

7. **Assignment of initiatives.** Every initiative needs a sponsor! The sponsor is committed to seeing the initiative through. They'll build the action plan and assemble the resources, including themselves, to get the initiative complete. If there isn't a person to jump at the initiative, it may not be something worth pursuing. In addition to assigning the sponsor, this is also the right time to establish commitments for when each initiative will be completed.

8. **Review the next steps.** You'll meet monthly to review progress on your plan, and every three months, that meeting

should include a full review of the strategic plan and open floor for adjustments, given any changes to the market or your business in the quarter. You must track your initiatives in a reliable tool that everyone is committed to updating. Software like Trello, Monday, and Asana is helpful for creating a visual tool for managing progress on your strategic plan, but a simple spreadsheet works just as well. These and any other next steps you've decided on should be reviewed with the team before ending the retreat.

Departmental Initiatives

Coming away from the retreat, the list of three to five initiatives per department now require detailed action plans associated with each. Within one month of the retreat, everyone with initiatives they're sponsoring should develop the detailed action plan for each initiative. Think of this as project planning by breaking the initiative down into its actionable steps with individual assignments and timelines attached to each action. It is important to note that the sponsor does not have to be the person responsible for taking all or even any of the action steps; they're simply the one responsible for ensuring the plan is developed, the steps are taken, and the initiative is successful. For example:

Initiative: Build with award-winning quality—Megan.
Action Steps:

- Form a quality committee: Jeff 10/15

- Quality committee to develop a comprehensive quality guideline: Jeff 12/15

  □ Formwork: Pedro 11/10

       ▫ Scaffolding: Ana 11/10

- Complete an assessment of our current quality against those standards: Megan 2/1

- Develop a training curriculum to address the gaps in our current assessment: Megan 5/1

- Train our trainers on our curriculum: Megan 6/1

- Launch the training program: Jeff 7/1

In our sample above, the final step of launching the training program is not going to be the final step on the initiative of building with award-winning quality, but it was as far into the future as Megan could see on the initiative. As things progress, timelines are hit, and the training program takes shape, Megan will revisit this initiative and add more items like hiring a QC manager and entering projects for award consideration. In the first month after the retreat, we just want each sponsor to plan out as far as they can see. We'll be reviewing and updating action items in our monthly, quarterly, and annual structures outlined in the next chapter.

Some initiatives do not fall clearly into one person's department. I typically put those items into a bucket for companywide initiatives. They can be assigned to anyone on the team who wishes to sponsor them. However, they commonly belong to one of the small number of top executives with companywide oversight, like the president or CEO.

Plan Documentation and Communication

Your goals must be believable to the organization, which means there must be a documented, actionable plan shared with the team. This is where so many visionary-type leaders fail. They believe their job stops at merely setting goals and inspiring the troops, but the troops are not inspired by goals without plans they understand and believe in. Instead, they'll be demoralized by an out-of-touch executive team with delusions of grandeur while they fear and resent the added pressure to accomplish something nobody believes in.

Plans are meant to be adapted to the market realities, and they're meant to be a daily playbook for decision-making. If you're regularly questioning the plan and wanting to take actions that aren't in the playbook, revisit the plan and consider whether it needs a tweak. While each sponsor is compiling their detailed action plans described in the previous section, someone from the retreat team must compile a documented strategic plan. This should be a document with these sections:

1. A detailed company vision that describes the goals of the business three years ahead

2. The core values that will guide the company on our journey to realizing the three-year vision

3. Our SWOT analysis for context on the initiatives section

4. The strategic initiatives we're undertaking companywide and by department to realize the three-year vision and the logic behind each related to the vision, values, and SWOT

I find the documented strategic plan runs between ten to twenty pages, depending on the detail provided with each initiative. Shorter is better, but context is important. I recommend writing it all out and having a professional edit the document.

Once the strategic plan is documented, it's ready for showtime. Spend a few bucks and have it bound into a spiral notebook or something similar. Get enough copies for everyone on your team, and hold a companywide meeting (or series of regional/local ones) to introduce the plan to your people. Present each element to the team, inviting them into the vision of your future and the important role each must play in it. Spend considerable time on the core values in this forum, talking about each and highlighting stories of these core values in action. This is an opportunity to align and inspire your entire company behind an exciting shared vision of the future. Capitalize on that. Review progress on the strategic plan with the whole company in an annual company celebration. Reference the strategic plan, and clearly show the company's commitment to seeing it through by identifying specific progress and recognizing those who contribute.

Many owners resist distributing the strategic plan. While I do agree there's a risk of it falling into the hands of your competition, unless you have some notable enemies in the market, I think this risk is minimal. At worst, it may motivate your competitors to work on their company in a similar fashion. Keep bottom-line financial performance metrics out of the documented strategic plan for distribution. If your executive team's plan has those metrics, produce a clean version for distribution.

CHAPTER 7

Execute the Plan

Review Progress on the Strategic Plan

Building the plan is the easy part! Execution is everything, and it's the place where most companies fall down. To prevent your strategic plan from gathering dust over the next three years while you're too busy to look up, I recommend setting up a structure to help you follow through. Some things in your construction business demand your time and attention to where there's no escaping them. Angry customer calls, surprise employee departures, accidents on the jobsite, and important bid deadlines are all examples of things you and your executive team probably don't struggle to find time to deal with. Moving your strategic plan forward is not one of those things. Not by a long shot. Quite the opposite, most items in your strategic plan are things nobody is pounding on your door demanding you deliver. The majority are items that only your executive team are paying attention to. If these items are left to be addressed like the other items your team confronts daily, they will be the last thing to get done … if they're lucky enough to get done at all. Set the expectation that spending time strategically working on the business plan is a part of the top responsibilities for your executives—two to four hours per week at a minimum. And set rules for what to do if someone isn't doing their part. Make sure everyone agrees early in the process: "If anyone does not do their part in moving forward the strategic plan, we will call them out for it. We won't feel bad or nervous to say something. We are all buying into executing this plan and can feel comfortable holding each other accountable. Do we all agree?"

Like scheduling appointments for a physical, dental cleaning, or personal trainer workout, the only way these nonurgent items will be completed is if you set aside the time to focus on them. It's crucial to schedule appointments with your executive team to talk about progress on the strategic plan rather than the countless other items the team is thinking about and working on. There are three environments for reviewing progress on your strategic plan: monthly progress meetings, quarterly strategy reviews, and annual retreats. Let's review the structure for each and make it easy for you to implement them.

MONTHLY PROGRESS MEETINGS

Each month, you and your department heads should meet solely to check the status of the strategic plan. There are other forums to discuss urgent items with the business, so keep this meeting on topic. Remember, you're also holding a monthly financial meeting, telling you about the health of your business, so don't let this meeting turn into that one. The monthly strategic plan review meeting should be completed in under an hour when the team is being accountable to their commitments. The agenda is:

1. Review the vision, mission, and values to set the tone (ten minutes)

2. Initiative review (twenty to fifty minutes)

   □ Each department head presents the status on their initiatives for the quarter and the action items for each initiative in the month ahead.

   □ Help from the team is requested and offered as each action item is presented.

QUARTERLY STRATEGY REVIEWS

Once every three months, in addition to the normal monthly progress meeting agenda, there should be a deeper review of the strategic plan, considering the ever-changing market and company conditions. The meeting should be four hours or less. This is the right forum to discuss things like the impact of staff additions and departures on the strategic plan. It is also an opportunity to put timely issues on the table that may take precedent over other, previously planned initiatives. The agenda should be:

1. Monthly agenda (sixty minutes)

2. Internal review (thirty minutes)

   □ Are there any emerging strengths we should leverage as a part of the strategic plan?

      » Gather the list—don't spend more than one minute per topic.

   □ Are there any emerging weaknesses we should fix as a part of the strategic plan?

» Gather the list—don't spend more than one minute per topic.

3. External review (thirty minutes)

   ▫ Are there any emerging opportunities we should capitalize on as a part of the strategic plan?

     » Gather the list—don't spend more than one minute per topic.

   ▫ Are there any emerging threats we should neutralize as a part of the strategic plan?

     » Gather the list—don't spend more than one minute per topic.

4. Issue processing (sixty minutes)

   ▫ Prioritize the list of topics gathered from the internal and external reviews.

     » Discuss each issue, creating action items and new initiatives as needed.

5. Set initiatives for the quarter (sixty minutes)

   ▫ Based on the existing strategic plan, review the initiatives you had planned for the quarter ahead, compare that list with any new initiatives that surfaced through issue processing, and commit to this quarter's initiatives as a group.

ANNUAL RETREATS

Once every four quarters, the quarterly meeting will be a full day to accommodate the annual strategy session. The annual meeting includes the quarterly agenda in addition to a year-in-review and yearly goal-setting discussion. This is a great time to recognize one another's accomplishments, reflect on shortcomings, and ensure lessons are learned that make the year ahead better than the last. The agenda is:

1. Last year in review (two hours)

    □ Each person presents what they're most proud of accomplishing, the biggest lesson they learned, and someone whose performance they want to recognize.

2. Goal-setting for the year ahead (two hours)

    □ Review performance targets for the year ahead.

    □ Each department head presents their departmental plan for the year ahead.

3. Quarterly agenda (four hours)

Update the Strategic Plan

Once your plan is built, it's important to trust in the preparation and hard work that went into building. It should prevent you from making too many modifications along the way. When companies lurch from one direction to the next by changing course depending on what the numbers say from month to month, the executive team's engagement wanes, trust in the plan fades, and the mention of the strategic plan become a laugh line around the company. All this is to say: Be disciplined. Stick to the plan. Avoid adding, subtracting, or altering it too often, or you risk undermining the integrity of your plan and all the effort that went into building it in the first place. With that said, there are reasonable accommodations to be made to allow you the ability to update the plan. If the plane is flying directly into the mountain, but the flight plan seems to have called for it, the pilot should throw out the flight plan and pull up, for God's sake.

There are three appropriate times to update the strategic plan and make necessary changes midstream. First, you might call up an emergency meeting topic because of some important change to your business or the market. Plans shouldn't be updated outside of quarterly or annual environments unless something is happening that demands you adjust your strategy immediately. The COVID-19 pandemic, for example, was a perfect example of something that would have demanded a look at your strategic plan to consider modifications, mostly temporary ones, to navigate the complexities that arose, from enhanced safety procedures to accommodating virtual workers and securing PPP funds to insulate the business from financial hardship. A member of the executive team leaving the company, a crash in the stock market or a key business sector for your business, or another strategically vital circumstance would call for an emergency strategy meeting. Often, the output of these meetings will not be a wholesale revision of the three-year plan but some interim strategic initiatives designed to mitigate a threat or capitalize on a time-sensitive opportunity that would change your business results in either a very bad or good way.

Building Operational Excellence

Absolutely nothing you do as a construction company matters as much as your ability to produce a project that meets the scheduling, budgetary, and quality expectations of your own business. The departments within your business responsible for delivering projects on time, within budget, and at your quality standard compose the definition of operations. Contractors are all made differently, but in general, you probably have your operations made up of project management, field operations, and estimating. You may also layer in design or fabrication to the extent you're designing, manufacturing, assembling, or otherwise preparing material for installation in the field. If, by chance, your operations are set up to include other departmental functions, I apologize for failing to capture that here. In future volumes, I can incorporate more nuances into this chapter with your feedback.

Operationally excellent contractors have no problem retaining clients and winning their next projects. They seem to operate like well-oiled machines, handling all manner of project types and creating consistently positive outcomes. They have certainty about the financial performance of their projects from the time they're in the preconstruction phase, and they have the confidence to price aggressively when they need to because the risk of failure is low. When markets tighten, operationally excellent companies can afford to take work at low gross profit margins. When markets open up, they're making considerably more than their sloppy competition, allowing them to squirrel away even more for that rainy day. If you're operationally excellent today, you're not worried about meeting the budget or schedule for the work you are pursuing or performing. Instead, you expect to beat both.

The only risks you face are trouble customers or underperforming subs and suppliers who get in your way. We talk about how to handle both those challenges elsewhere, so in this section, we'll focus on how to strive for and achieve operational excellence so you can have the confidence and peace of mind that comes with knowing you're set up to win on every project.

CHAPTER 8

Embrace Process

Imagine you are the plant manager at a Coca-Cola manufacturing and bottling plant. Your job is to ensure a consistent soft drink is made, bottled, boxed, and made ready to ship. Over 1.9 billion servings of Coke are consumed around the world each year, and each is made to the specifications demanded by the geographic market they're in. If you know anyone who is a true Coca-Cola devotee, they can spot the difference between Coke and a knockoff in an instant. As plant manager, how do you produce your share of almost two billion servings of a product that consistently meets the extraordinarily discerning demands of a cultlike following of consumers?

Load it with high fructose corn syrup and caffeine so they get addicted! Wait, no, sorry.

The answer we're looking for is that you ensure every step of production and packaging is down to an ironclad process that cannot fail. You install quality control measures that double-check the product before it leaves your facility just on the nano-chance that something could be off. Thanks to modern technologies, your processes are also automated and perfected to remove any shadow of imperfection from the product. In this way, you keep headquarters off your back and your customers happy, if less healthy, and coming back for more.

Now let's imagine one of your shift managers is a creative type. He's smart and experienced, having worked for another soft drink company for twenty years. He deviates from the process and tries to improve production volume using tricks he's picked up over the years. His finished product is less consistent than the standard, but he's getting more production than any other manager. How do you handle that? Simply mandate he returns to the processes you have in place, and you destroy the large volume of inconsistent products. Then you may call HQ and share the concept with them and see if they have any interest in some of the volume-boosting techniques your shift manager demonstrated. HQ will either embrace the change, installing a new process for the whole facility, or they'll shoot it down, and everyone must move on. It is OK for the company to make the determination that production volume is more important than consistency (though I'd advise against it), but it is definitely not OK for your plant to have inconsistent processes.

I use this scenario because it's so obvious how critical consistent processes are to the functioning of this kind of business. When we consider the possibility of allowing a single person to deviate from the processes, we can clearly see this is not a good choice for the business. As helpful as this analogy is, we need to recognize that construction is not as controlled an environment as a manufacturing facility that produces the same product repeatedly. Despite massive advancements in, and an industry-wide trend toward, off-site fabrication, volumetric, and modular approaches to construction, which bring more controlled manufacturing to the construction environment, humans' varied appetite for structure design and differentiation will not disappear anytime soon. We're not going to reduce construction complexity down to something like bottling a soft drink in our lifetime. I do strongly recommend exploring how your company can embrace these trends, however, and we'll get into that in the chapter "Running Up the Score." For the purposes of this chapter, we'll focus on the importance of processes, regardless of your current production and operations.

Core and Supporting Processes and Subprocesses

There are various repetitive tasks that your organization does in pursuit of the same set of outcomes every day, week, or month. These tasks, stacked together, amount to processes. The first order of processes are core processes. You have a core process to (1) find opportunities, (2) estimate them, (3) win them, (4) plan how to complete them, (5) systematically complete them, (6) get paid for completing them, and (7) ensure your customer is happy and wants to provide you with another opportunity in the future.

You also must perform supporting processes that enable your company to perform its core process. For example, to make sure you have a team capable of performing the core function, you must (1) identify staff needs, (2) recruit to fill positions, (3) select the right candidates, (4) train new hires to perform in their roles, (5) advance their skills to meet the demands of your core function, and (6) ensure your employees are happy and want to stay with your company.

Within each task within the processes outlined above, a series of steps must be taken within that process that we'll call subprocesses. For example, to perform step 3 (estimating) of your core process, you must: (1) review the plans to understand the broad scope of the project, (2) create the estimate in your estimating software, (3) perform takeoffs, (4) prepare a list of RFIs and get them answered, and (5) contact subs and suppliers for pricing on defined scopes, etc.

CORE PROCESSES	Find Opportunities →	Estimate →	Sell
SUB-PROCESSES	Market research Opportunity tracking CRM management	Plan review Set up in estimation software Takeoffs RFIs Secure Pricing	Initial opportunity qualification Prepare presentation Conduct scope review Negotiate construct terms Turnover to operations

SUPPORTING PROCESSES	Staffing	Financial Reporting	Information Technology
SUB-PROCESSES	Identify staff needs Recruit candidates Select candidates Train new hires	WIP reports P&L Balance sheet Projections	Personal device setup Software stack management Help desk procedures

I'm sure your processes will diverge from the samples provided above, but they are certain to exist. The questions are: Have you clearly defined your processes, and is your team performing each task in a consistent way? For most construction companies, the answer is no. The results for most construction companies are, unsurprisingly, highly inconsistent from project to project and from team to team. Construction companies lacking defined, replicable processes suffer from, among other things:

1. An inability to identify the root causes of profit fade from project to project

2. An overreliance on a handful of highly capable people in key positions

3. The inability to hire and develop talent from within

4. Inaccurate or nonexistent profit projections

5. A teams, B teams, and C teams

6. Poor safety records

7. Inconsistent product and service quality

8. A culture of blame and favoritism

Documenting Processes

Documenting processes for your organization may seem like a daunting task, and let's not mince words: it is a lot of work. Don't let that stop you! The rewards are too great and too lasting to allow a lot of work to slow you down. WBCCs take on big tasks all the time. They embrace the challenge and find the sense of accomplishment rewarding. Like any major undertaking, documenting the processes you follow for your organization is best approached by breaking it down into pieces and making consistent progress over a defined period. Notice I say "document your processes" rather than "build" them. While it may be true that you do not have a process for some things in your organization, it is almost certain that you have a lot more processes than you think. What you probably don't have is those processes clearly documented, which makes it hard to teach and manage them. And if you can't teach and manage your processes, you can't effectively grow your business, hand down succession, etc. Documenting a process that you already have in your head does not take much time. What it takes is a format you like and the ability to tune out distractions for thirty to sixty minutes at a time.

The place to start is with the processes you already have but don't have documented. First, lay out the core, supporting, and subprocesses, as outlined above. You can do this on a large whiteboard, on notebook paper, or using software (I like Lucidchart for this purpose). Then, simply identify each process for which you already clearly know how you want things done. Don't worry about the processes that need to be built at this point ... we'll get to those later. Just make progress by documenting the processes you can so you can take a bite out of this project.

When documenting the processes themselves, I use simple outline formatting provided in many word-processing software programs, but I know people who need the visual representations provided by flowcharts. Whatever your preference, know this: you can always repackage the way your processes are presented to your people, but you must first get the processes out of your head, so do not let yourself get stuck because you're aiming for perfection in the documentation step.

Once you've documented all the processes you already had in your head, it's time to refer to the process chart and identify those that need to be built and prioritize them. Unlike the intent of the initial documentation step, which was to get all the known processes documented so we could make significant progress on the project of process documentation, in this step we prioritize which processes we need in place the most because the intent is to fill in the process gaps where your company is feeling the lack of process the most. For example, one subcontracting company I helped noticed that their projects were consistently missing profit expectations. They had good estimating processes and field production processes in place, but they were weak on project management processes, relying too heavily on a couple of long-tenured employees to know what they were doing. They had grown the PM staff and began experiencing major inconsistencies. This profit fade is what the company was experiencing, and the most obvious need for processes was in project management, so that's where they started.

Now for building new processes, there are three avenues down which you can go. You can:

1. Build your custom processes from scratch.

2. Find a consultant or specialist in the area you're lacking a process and have them build a custom process with you.

3. Lean on peer relationships in the industry and see whether anyone you trust and respect has processes you can adopt and adapt.

My recommendation is choice three. That's coming from someone who has been a construction industry consultant for more than a decade, building custom processes alongside clients. It is more time and cost-effective to adopt and adapt processes than it is to piece it together yourself or pay a consultant to do it with you. Someone else has been there before, and you might as well benefit from their hard work. You can reciprocate by sharing your hard work on the processes you had in your head.

When building processes on your own, be honest with yourself about whether you have the knowledge to develop a solid process in this field. Would you be making it up with no demonstrated proof of concept? If so, consider the consultant or peer. If, however, you know enough to be dangerous, building your own processes from scratch can be a rewarding experience. You get the chance to dream up your unique approach, do some targeted research to explore the latest trends, and truly differentiate yourself from your competition. If you want all the benefits of that level of customization but you know you're not qualified to build on your own, it's best to seek a consultant for the project.

Visit www.wellbuiltconsulting.com to learn more about bringing a consultant onto your project.

A critical note: Whichever path you take as you develop documented processes for every area of your business, engage key team members in the areas of their expertise along the way. The processes you're documenting will directly affect your employees daily. To waste an epic amount of time documenting processes you never see implemented in your business, go ahead and do all this project work without engaging the people you will turn to for implementation. By bringing in your key staff's input, not only will you improve your chances of implementing the processes once they're built, but you'll also improve the speed of documentation by spreading the workload around. One client completed a massive process documentation effort in an impressive sixty-day period by pulling each one of their department leaders into the effort. The VP of operations, VP of estimating, general superintendent, director of HR, controller, and president (owner) each took the processes in their respective areas of expertise and followed the recommendations outlined in this chapter to get all their processes documented in record time. Each team member spent an average of forty hours completing the project, and they collaborated as needed with outside consultants and peer group members to get it done. There was also a healthy amount of dialogue within each department with their team members to get feedback as the processes were being developed. Not only did they build the processes in two months, but they also had them implemented within six months thereafter. An incredible amount of focus and support from the culture made this possible, while the resulting efficiency and quality made the efforts more than worthwhile.

Zooming back out to the entire project of building and documenting processes for your company, once you (1) document the processes you have, and (2) build the processes you're missing in a prioritized fashion, it is time to (3) build training to make sure the processes can be implemented, and (4) supervise their consistent use.

Training and Implementing Processes

Your new documented processes will take the place of whatever the team has been doing, if they were doing anything at all, in that area before your process was developed. So the biggest challenge you'll face in implementing new processes is the behavior change it will require. Let's think about implementing processes and the corresponding behavior change on a spectrum.

On one side of the spectrum, many processes you had in your head were already being followed by your team in some form or fashion, and the documentation of the processes formalized something they were already doing. Implementing these processes requires very little behavior change … tweaks, if anything.

In the middle of the spectrum, you have created documented processes for actions your team has been performing in a different way or in a way that varied from person to person on your team. Implementing these processes requires some convincing that the newly documented processes are preferable to what the team is doing. This will take open discussions, training, and perhaps one-on-one coaching with hard cases.

On the other end of the spectrum, you'll have some entirely new processes for things the team has never done before but that you want them to do. Implementing these processes requires you to show the need to do the new thing at all. Once people have bought into the need to do something new, they'll need training and coaching to learn and practice the new standard.

All processes should have corresponding training to ensure current and future team members understand them and can execute them. Even those processes already essentially being followed should be trained. Take nothing for granted, and remind the team there is always something to improve as they undergo reinforcement training on processes they already know. Let's be clear about training: telling people the process does not constitute training. Telling is not training. Training should be created with behavior change in mind. Process implementation training should include:

1. Proof this process is needed—typically by showing what would happen in the absence of a process or when the process is done the wrong way.

2. A clear overview of the process.

3. An in-depth description and demonstration of each step.

4. An opportunity to challenge and discuss the process.

5. Practice and testing.

Once someone has gone through training, it's helpful to just create training videos or manuals with the process overview and the description and demonstration of each step for reference. The thing I'm stressing here, though, is that if you want to see your processes implemented, you'll create a training environment with each element that lets your team go through the experience of changing the way they think and, therefore, act. With a team of people who have learned the philosophies that guide your processes, the YouTube-style how-to reference material acts as a good reminder from day to day.

It is one thing to build training sessions, and it's yet another to deliver them. People who are bored or confused due to poor training delivery will struggle to focus and engage for long enough to learn. Consider sending select team members out to receive training on public speaking before asking them to deliver your training. Depending on your company's size, consider hiring someone full time to lead your training programs. They don't need to be the subject matter expert running the session alone, but if they have the skills to connect with an audience and engage them, you can pair them with an expert on the topic for training.

Training shouldn't happen once. It is not an event; it is a discipline. One client provides four hours of training every Friday. Every new employee (within their first year) attends every week. They learn about things that immediately pertain to their role, but they also receive cross-training on skills and processes that pertain to other roles. In this way, a new hire—regardless of their experience—receives about two hundred hours of training (10 percent of their time on the job) in structured training environments in their first year. In addition, tenured employees are expected to attend at least one Friday training block per month, so even the veterans get close to fifty hours of formal training (2 percent of their time on the job) in structured training environments every year. Consider what your training programming should look like to support all the processes you build and want to implement.

With the team trained on each of your processes and ongoing reinforcement training in place to ingrain the concepts into the fabric of the culture, supervise their consistent implementation. If you think back to the "Measure What Matters" chapter, you'll recall measuring leading indicators. There is perhaps no better leading indicator than confirming our team is consistently following the processes we believe will lead to success. If we can prove that the team, companywide, did everything today in the exact way we've drawn it up, our lagging indicators will follow in a positive way.

Capturing proof of process compliance is easier said than done. However, some hacks can allow us visibility without micromanaging. My favorite way of monitoring process implementation is to weave the use of smart tools into executing the process itself. In this way, following the process requires the use of a tool that will automatically capture the proof of process implementation. An example might be creating a material-stocking checklist in your project management software that guides your foreperson in the process for material stocking while requiring them to confirm that each step of the process is completed and take photos to confirm each step. It's a helpful tool in that your foreperson can follow along and make sure they're not missing anything, but it also captures data to run reports and confirm the team is following the processes as intended. Staying with this example, if you ran a weekly report and could confirm that every project was stocked with materials in the exact way the process dictates, you could know with a level of certainty that your scheduled installations would move forward as planned. Wherever possible, do not require your people to fill out reports, but instead, require your people to use tools that will help them execute their processes, and pull your reports out of these tools. This way, you'll get the visibility you need to effectively supervise that things are happening the way they must without creating inefficiencies and frustration caused by extra reporting for a team of people just trying to get their jobs done.

Not everything can be supervised using a smart technological tool that captures the data you need, however. For those things, managers in every department of WBCCs must be ready to inspect what they expect by spending some hands-on time supervising their teams. Taking the time to regularly observe your teams at work will offer great visibility into additional training needs and give your managers the opportunity to address issues now, on the job, which can often be the thing a team member needs to go from knowing to owning a process. Supervisors who haven't actually watched their people perform the tasks they're responsible for are missing the opportunity to coach and course-correct. They claim they're too busy dealing with fires. Make your managers stop fighting fires for long enough to diagnose the source of the heat and prevent future fires!

Optimizing Processes

It can be a painful thought, but once you have all your processes documented, training built to support them, and supervisory structures in place to track their implementation, you still must be open to changing your processes. Things change, you'll continue to learn things, your people will innovate, and you must be ready to accept positive changes to your processes if you wish to be at your best. WBCCs have this awareness, and while they maintain strict adherence to their processes, they also encourage innovative ideas within their companies. If a team member—*any* team member—has an idea for how a process can be improved, it should be heard out. If the idea has merit, a test group should compare methods. The best method will be adopted, and if that is the new method, that process will be documented and trained, while the supervisory structures must be adjusted to account for this new process. This is what optimization looks like. While the heaviest lifting of embracing processes is behind us, once we have them all documented and the training in place, WBCCs never accept the status quo when there could be a better way of doing things we can embrace. Not only will it improve the business, but it will also show your employees their input and make them feel more engaged in process execution!

As you measure your lagging indicators, you will continue to identify measurements that are not good enough. Working to find the root causes of these poor metrics will further identify processes needing optimization ... or even, perhaps, creation. For example, one client documented their client communication processes, trained them, and supervised their implementation. All was in order, but their win rate with customers was not improving after over a year of consistent implementation. They sought my help to reevaluate the process; I found key modifications, and we plugged it back in. They retrained staff and modified the supervisory structures, and we measured. A year later, we were seeing consistent upticks in their win rates with existing clients, and that trend has continued.

Design the Business Like You Would a Building

Imagine sitting down to design yourself a building as an investment. The first thing you'd ask yourself is what function that building had to perform. Are you housing people or providing a place to work? What kind of work will occur there? The point is, you'd better know what purpose you want the building to serve. Once you had figured that out, you would determine a budget for the building, and you'd design the building the best way you knew how to accomplish the purpose you had in mind within budget. You'd select the best materials for the application within the budget and specify them in the design. That's how you design a building that will satisfactorily serve your purposes.

What you wouldn't do is look around your yard and garage and ask yourself, "What can I build with all the stuff I have here?" and expect that to pan out. Yet this is what most owners of contracting companies are doing with their businesses each day. Your people are the materials, and your business is the building. Instead of designing your organizational structure to meet your vision, you try to make things work without changing roles or people to better suit needs. You've got unfinished plywood as exterior cladding and tile where there should be concrete. You're running a switchgear that can't fully power the building, and there aren't any faucets in the building at all! This is what it's like to have people miscast in roles they can't handle and key positions missing from your organizational chart altogether. The building is not working, and nobody will happily occupy the place! As a contractor, have you ever looked at a set of plans and had to scratch your head in disbelief at the flawed decision-making that went into the choices? That's what someone like me does when they look at your organizational chart's design and the people you have in those roles!

When you are designing your organizational structure, it is important to first set the people aside. Stop trying to think of the right role for Judy. I know you care about Judy, and we'll get to that next, but you're designing the ideal building here, and you can't be too worried about the materials you have. Design the business to do what it needs to do by defining the roles and responsibilities first. For a contractor, the functions you will have fit into these three main categories:

- **How you get work**

  - Preconstruction: How you provide a consulting service to your clients that improves your chances of winning the work

  - Estimating: How you produce correct cost estimates for what it will take to build the work and determine a pricing strategy so you can win and be profitable

  - Business development: How you build and maintain relationships with clients and partners to increase the work you win and the rate at which you win it

  - Sales: How you position your company to win the work you've brought in and estimated

  - Marketing: How you build awareness about your company to improve your chances of winning the right work

- **How you build the work you get**

  - Labor (if applicable): How you build the work

  - Project management: How you provide the field and fabrication what they need as well as plan and track the work you're building

  - Field management: How you ensure you build the work safely, correctly, and on time

  - Fabrication (if applicable): How you construct or assemble the materials you install

- **How you support the team getting the work**

  - Accounting: How you track and flow all the money generated by doing the work

  - Human resources: How you hire and keep the resources needed to get, build, and support the work

  - IT: How you ensure the team has the technological tools they need to succeed in getting, building, and supporting the work

  - Facilities: How you ensure the team has a work environment conducive to successfully getting, building, and supporting the work

  - Fleet management: How you ensure the team has the equipment needed to build the work

  - Warehouse: How you prepare and protect the materials necessary to build the work

  - Distribution: How you get the materials to the team in time to build the work

While there is no universally accepted way of structuring a construction company, there are key decisions you'll need to make as you design your ideal "building." Will you have the sales, estimating, and project management functions handled by the same role? Are you ready for a CFO, or do you need a controller? When must you hire HR in-house? Will you hire business developers or assign BD responsibilities to the whole team? Will you self-perform the scope or subcontract everything? Do you need a general superintendent? All these questions and more must be answered in a thoughtful way that is specific to your business. I've seen successful outcomes using too many different organizational structures to offer any rules for doing this beyond what I've shared here. The key is to ensure the vision for your business and your core values will be served by selecting a certain design.

For example, a large general contractor with a vision to rank in the top three in every local market they serve has an extensive culture of entrepreneurship. Their organization is designed to match. They are mostly decentralized, placing considerable trust with local leadership in each market to run their business unit in alignment with their values. It works for them, but it would not work for a different vision with different values.

Instead of prescribing a certain approach to organizational design, I'll provide some principles for you to consider for your operational functions in estimating, project management, and field management. These should help you make decisions on designing your organizational chart and more on your journey toward operational excellence.

CHAPTER 9

Excellence in Estimating

Successful estimating is a knife's edge between winning too much low-margin work and winning too little work due to high pricing. It's a function that will make or break your construction business. A great estimating function will lead to strong sales volume at a price that sets your team up to make a reasonable profit. If the estimating function is weak, you are in trouble one way or another. To reduce risk, multiple people must thoroughly understand your estimating function, which must be memorialized as a documented process and updated regularly.

A $50 million general contractor was experiencing a losing streak on bids. A little over a year before, a new chief estimator was hired from outside the company to replace the previous chief estimator, who quit suddenly. A year in, they were averaging an 8 percent win ratio under his tenure, with customer feedback that their pricing was too high, and they were getting desperate to win work. The group, which was used to winning about 25 percent of their bids, was shaken by this disturbance. Trying to get to the bottom of it, they grilled their subcontractors about whether they had been awarded the losing projects with another GC. Often, they were. How was this possible? If their subs were on these projects with other GCs, how were they being beaten so consistently on price? One valuable and very direct subcontractor had the courage to say, "We never give you the real price on bid day … you always come to us for another 5 percent in buyout, so we price your projects 5 percent higher to account for what we need to make." This was what the GC needed to hear to break free from their slump. The new chief estimator took over the pricing strategy and did not understand this persistent issue when submitting bids. With the long-term plan of correcting relationships with subs who were padding their numbers, they began correctly adjusting their pricing strategy to match the actual prices their subs were providing. Their hit rate rose back to its 25 percent standard, and they produced the work profitably.

The Mission of Estimating

The mission of the estimating function should be to develop an accurate projection of the actual costs you will incur to build a project and to do so in time to meet deadlines set by the customer. Nothing more and nothing less will do. This accurate projection gives the business the information it needs to determine the appropriate GP target for the project. Pricing strategy is a different skill set from estimating. It requires an understanding of current market conditions, customer relationships, vendor relationships, and your backlog and resource availability for the time the project is slated to go. In WBCCs, the role of establishing your pricing strategy may be performed by individual estimators, but that should be done only if the estimator is qualified. More often, the pricing strategy is driven by the executive level.

In the story above, estimating could not project actual costs. Their projected costs were higher than those their subcontractors were ready to provide. The causes—companies that had learned to pad their numbers on bid day when bidding to this GC, and a lack of institutional knowledge or structure left behind by the previous department head—were just two of many causes that can lead estimating departments to get it wrong. Inaccurate takeoffs, bad unit pricing or labor assumptions, mistakes and typos with the estimating system, and poor vendor or sub coverage are some others. Confirming that the estimating department produces accurate cost projections should be your first and most critical task as you work through this chapter. Getting it right requires looking at estimating as a part of a broader system.

Estimating as a Part of a Broader System

Estimating leads to project management, which leads to field management, so it must not be considered cut off from the rest of operations. Estimating is the first phase of operations, not separate from it. That doesn't necessarily mean estimating belongs under the purview of your head of the operations department, though. As stated, there are many successful ways of structuring your construction business. The key is maintaining the mindset and commitment to viewing estimating as a part of the broader operations system at work in your business. To ensure estimates truly reflect the cost of building your projects, you must share lessons learned from project management and the field back with estimating so they can update their approach to reflect reality better. This can be done by instituting after-action reviews (AARs) upon the completion of every project, which allows the team responsible for putting the work in place to improve iteratively. The

AAR comes from the military's commitment to review and learn from every operation. Applied to construction, the best practice is to capture lessons learned from the field and PM staff throughout construction and bring all those to a meeting at the end designed to share intelligence across departments and improve moving forward. So, for example, when field management tells your estimating team that a specific feature of work could not be built as estimated, that information can be captured, and you can update the estimating tools to reflect this new data. Taking this AAR approach turns every project into an opportunity to improve.

Org Structure for Estimating

Depending on the size and structure of your company, estimating may be a function performed by estimators or by project managers. There are strengths and weaknesses to both approaches. Whichever approach you take to staffing your estimating function, you must also plan for and overcome the drawbacks.

Hybrid Estimator/PM Model

```
                    PM/ESTIMATE

    ┌─────────────────┬─────────────────┬─────────────────┐

  PROJECT 1          PROJECT 2          PROJECT 3
Pre-construction stage  Under construction  Under construction
```

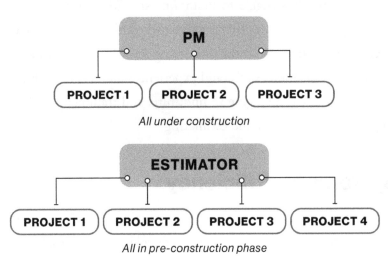

PM—Estimator division of labor model

PM

| PROJECT 1 | PROJECT 2 | PROJECT 3 |

All under construction

ESTIMATOR

| PROJECT 1 | PROJECT 2 | PROJECT 3 | PROJECT 4 |

All in pre-construction phase

There's much to be said for having project managers estimate the projects they'll eventually run. This approach can lead to a higher level of personal ownership of the estimating product, as the PM will naturally want to identify and proactively avoid potential estimating pitfalls that can cause them to fail when they're responsible for the project's financial performance. PMs who estimate have often told me they believe they are more likely to estimate the project by building it in their minds and on paper rather than approaching estimating as purely counting and pricing. However, while project managers tend to estimate with the construction phase in mind and that has benefits, that approach can also leave you overpriced due to an overly cautious operator developing the cost estimate.

There is also much to be said for having a dedicated estimating department remaining only focused on project pursuits and turning the project over to a PM once it is awarded. The division of labor provided by separating estimating and project management allows for deeper specialization in the art and science of estimating, which can translate into greater efficiency and quality. Project managers who estimate typically struggle to maintain estimating as a habit while managing a lot of work. This leads to awkward peaks and valleys in revenue while they restart the estimating machine when work slows down. Different tools, skills, and experiences are needed to fill each role, so it can be challenging to find, hire, and train people who can do project management and estimating.

Systems for Efficiency

It is common and positive to develop your own efficiency-creating formulas for estimating and pricing strategies, but never allow your team to become so dependent on the formulas that they lose the essence of their role: the accurate projection of costs to build a project. Many contractors wrongly have pricing strategies built into their estimating tools. Estimators perform takeoffs and plug their inputs into an estimating program, which produces a total price to submit. Voilà! As you're reading this, you may think, "What a great and efficient plan," and I understand why. However, when a machine determines your pricing strategy automatically, you must consider the ongoing irrelevance of the assumptions used to get to the price. How do we account for market conditions, client relationships, vendor relationships, and our need for that work to fill our schedule at the right time? When there's a discrepancy in the estimate, it's excruciating to uncover the problem underneath layers of formulas. WBCCs produce hard cost estimates broken down into each cost category; then they apply a pricing strategy.

Estimating must be a replicable, trainable science in your construction business. Typically for small to midsize contractors, a single estimating genius knows the secret recipe for estimating. Often, this person likes that the way it is. Perhaps it gives them some sense of comfort they can't be replaced, or it boosts their ego by making them feel important. It is a major risk for failure in your business if the person gets hit by a bus, and it's a bottleneck to growth if you can't replicate and train a system. Document your estimating process down to the smallest detail. Ideally, this should happen in partnership with your current estimating genius, but hire a consultant to do it for you if they're not interested in helping. Reward your helpful genius! Pay them more to train and develop other people to be as great as they, and if they're suited to it, they can emerge as a leader in the company.

Finding the Gaps

All of estimating will revolve around your review of plans and translating the design into a price to construct. A common complaint from the construction community is the lack of complete and coordinated plans. Though I have some great success stories about design/build and IPD relationships overcoming this issue together, A/E issues are beyond the scope of this book ... maybe next time. I'll call the problems you find in the plans "gaps." These gaps are where most contractors are either making or losing money. If you fail to find the gaps, your price could be too high (you lose) or too low (you win but eventually lose). If you find the gaps, what should you do? The answer is so incredibly nuanced and dependent on the circumstances that we can't get into it completely. However, I will offer an idea for GCs and another for specialty contractors to consider.

If you're a GC, your client probably wants to know the gaps so there aren't surprise costs or battles later. It's their money, after all. Your team and others may find gaps left by your subs. A strong GC can be firm with their client, educate them about gaps, and prepare them for the added costs of failing to catch surprises. Even when you're still competing for a project, this transparent approach can work. Remind them that catching surprises now is much preferred to catching them while under construction and bringing the project to a grinding halt. Resist the temptation to tell your client what they want to hear. Fight before the project gets underway, and they'll forget about the fight by the time the project is complete, and they are a happy customer.

If you're a specialty contractor, how you handle the gaps is a question of ethics and strategy. Many subs will be silent about gaps they believe will lead to significant change orders for them later. This lets them reduce the first costs they show the GC and owner, increasing their likelihood of winning the project. It also puts them on a collision course for a significant change order battle later in the project. Personally, I hate this approach because it violates my ethical standards, but I understand how it happens and how good people rationalize it. The specialty contractor has learned that they often only win by being low on bid day or even after if there are dreaded rounds of best and final offers (BAFOs). They need the work and view it as a necessary evil to withhold valuable information from their client and the owner. I have found that an acceptable compromise is to bring gaps to the GC verbally and ask the GC if they want you to correct the scope in your pricing and submit an RFI, or price what's in the plans. That allows you to be ethical by bringing it up to your client, leaving the decision of what to bring to their owner to them. Ideally, they'll ask you to explain and price the gap, then advocate for your company on the project due to your skill in spotting the gaps and ethical approach to handling it. Overall, we must strive as an industry to fix broken procurement norms that reward dishonesty in the first place, but again … that's a subject for a different book.

Excellence in Project Management

The PM function has three key responsibilities. First, the PM is ultimately responsible for the project's financial performance. Their job is to ensure the project meets or outperforms the estimated cost and budget metrics. Second, they are one of the client's most important relationships with the company and must keep customers happy throughout construction. Third, they must service the team in the field to ensure they have what they need to succeed. Strong project managers can perform miracles. They touch so many parts of the project, letting them make a huge impact. It all starts with the hard facts: the project metrics.

Mastery of the Metrics

Your company may measure a host of metrics during construction, and if you're using the data well, that's great! The foundational elements for a PM are schedule and budget. The PM should always know where the project stands on both metrics in something close to real time. That requires a set of habits beginning with job setup and flowing daily throughout the project.

Tracking schedule and budget can be done with a weekly habit of visiting each project in the field or shop to assess its progress against the master schedule. Are we ahead or behind? Are we in sequence? Each week the PM should produce their assessment of the percentage completed on each feature of work. This should be compared with both the schedule and actual costs to confirm that we are on track in both metrics. In addition to tracking progress in the construction phase, the PM must ensure vendors and subcontractors are ready to meet deadlines to keep the team on track. Having and managing a materials submittal log showing necessary approval dates for every material based on lead time is another best practice that falls into the PM's zone of responsibility.

CORRECTIVE MEASURES FOR BAD METRICS

What happens when the metrics are off? First, if they're maintaining the weekly habits described above and they are qualified to perform the project management function, you shouldn't be off by much in either area by the time the problem is caught. Finding out about schedule and budget issues on projects weeks or months after going off course is a strong sign of either a lack of good habits or a significant gap in competence at the PM level. They could be the wrong person or need focused training and development.

So assuming you've caught it early, a huddle should immediately occur with the right people to discuss the issue. PMs should not feel they must solve everything independently, as the right call may be to pull in more senior staff. This is one of the most common errors of people in the PM function. They rightly feel a sense of personal ownership for the project's success but wrongly think they must resolve all problems independently. Instead, the PM should leverage the right resource for the situation. When a problem arises, it's all hands on deck, and all resources are on the table for the PM. The PM should also document the sources of problems early and often, as the causes are often not theirs. While a collaborative demeanor should be maintained throughout, a PM is also responsible for protecting their company from damage caused by other entities or things outside of anyone's control.

The Company's Ambassador

When maintaining healthy relations with everyone outside the company, the ambassador role is an important part of the PM function. While most of an ambassador's role is collegial, sometimes an ambassador must use all the goodwill they've built to deal with difficult circumstances in a productive way. I use the term "healthy relations" here specifically because we must avoid war altogether. As anyone who has experienced a legal proceeding in the construction industry will attest, by the time lawyers are involved, you've lost more money than you stood to gain in the first place. Great PMs walk the tightrope between great customer service and protecting the company's financial interests. This magic trick requires incredible soft skills combined with acute attention to detail, a rare combination in one person. This person can build and maintain great relationships while being firm, when necessary, which is made much easier when supported by clearly demonstrated facts. For example, consider most of the change order fights you've been a part of. They typically root back to a lack of strong backup for the proposed change order or the lack of a positive relationship, which makes it easy for some clients to argue with even the best-supported evidence. The PM function must keep your clients coming back for more, not because you acquiesce to their demands but because you run a hell of a job.

Many PMs are also responsible for procuring subcontractors and vendors, but regardless of who handles this function in your business, this is an ambassador role as well. One of the most dysfunctional things in the building industry is procurement, starting with owners through the entire value chain. The way you buy says something about your company's culture and ethics.

What message are you sending when you partner with someone for months as they provide dozens of hours of free preconstruction support and you conduct a competitive bid, giving the project to their competitor for 2 percent less? Word of that kind of behavior travels and does as much damage to your business as an angry customer in the long run.

Servicing the Field and Shop

Before the project starts, the team counts on the PM for excellent planning. This amounts to collaborating with field operations to produce a master schedule, building a detailed budget for the project based on their own in-depth estimate, and completing all the necessary paperwork to ensure no snags hold up construction. Staying up to speed with design changes and adjusting to the resulting causes and effects to every detail is par for the course.

PMs must view the field and shop as their customer to support and service throughout construction. Only through them can the PM succeed, and while it's not theirs to manage, the PM must lead proactive communication with both, checking in to see how they can ease the way for construction and fabrication. In addition, they must continuously collaborate with their field supervisor counterpart to adapt the plan together based on the metrics and realities on site. A good collaboration between a PM and their field counterpart also considers individual strengths and weaknesses, letting everyone add value where they're most capable. Who is the best person to handle an angry client, for example? If the answer to these questions isn't clear, the PM owns it. The field and shop have work to fabricate and put in place.

CHAPTER 11

Excellence in Field Operations

Where the rubber meets the road is on the construction site in the hands of the people using their hands and tools to bring the plans to life. WBCCs invest generously in their field staff because they recognize these are the people who matter most to their business. No investment in the field is more important than providing them the training they need to perform at their best. A well-trained field can outperform estimated labor almost every time. If you're a GC, the same idea holds with superintendents. Those with deep construction expertise eliminate the causes of blown budgets like slowdowns, unsafe conditions, and rework by applying their knowledge across the subcontracting team. Contractors struggle with strategies to train their field in a cost-effective way. Have members of your leadership team dedicate a part of their time visiting jobsites and providing hands-on training in the field. When credible leaders in the company spend time in the field, it has the added benefit of boosting morale and employee loyalty.

Soft Skills for Field Management

In construction, *soft* and *field* are not words you often think of in the same sentence! However direct and assertive they need to be, the best field managers also have enough awareness to know when and how to turn on the charm. Superintendents and forepersons should learn the importance of adapting their communication styles to their audience and the situation at hand. Using angry tonality and language should happen extremely rarely, if at all. The same message can be conveyed much more effectively with calmer tones if combined with no-nonsense language and serious body language. When people feel attacked, they don't react well in general. That goes for employees and clients alike. Great field managers know how to get what they need right now and have the people they're talking to feel like they were asked, not told.

Planning in the Field

Without exception, there should be a morning huddle between on-site field managers and their staff. This daily discussion is when the field manager calls the plays, and the team must show they understand what is expected. This is also a great opportunity to recognize strong performance from the day before, provide a safety reminder, and set a positive tone for the day. In Monday's huddle, the field manager should paint a picture of success for the week, so the team is bought into making it happen. In addition to a morning huddle, the field manager should produce two-week look-ahead plans each week to think about their needs for materials, manpower, and support from the rest of the company to succeed.

It is crucial that the field is coordinated with the office on the two-week look-ahead, being collaborative and adaptable to meet company goals. WBCCs have open lines of communication with the field managers, their supervisors, and the PM team. Decisions affecting budget and schedule must be made collectively, which culturally means everyone's voice counts. This partnership between the field and office, when working correctly, will maintain total clarity in operations on every project and let your team beat their goals.

A Culture of Safety

Thankfully, there are countless valuable resources to help your team to learn habits and techniques to maintain a safe jobsite. Most contractors' safety programs incorporate best practices from OSHA and other resources into their own standards to ensure people go home safe at the end of every day. However, safety violations persist, and thousands of people are being hurt, maimed, and killed on construction sites in the United States every year. The difference for many is not the lack of safety training or knowledge, but the lens through which they're viewing safety programs. The mindset that safety protocols are a necessary evil is problematic. With that mindset, we're beginning from a place of resistance. It's like paying taxes. We wouldn't if we didn't have to, but we must, so we do. Well, how many people are looking for wiggle room on their taxes? Just a little? Everyone, right? If we take this mindset and apply it to safety in the field, we'll constantly have people trying to get away with as much as possible and shirking safety protocols.

The right mindset toward safety should be like putting our clothes on before leaving the house or turning the key in the ignition before we start the car. It's not something we wouldn't do if we didn't have to; instead, it is something you should want to do because it makes everything work better. Companies should treat safety violations like they would if someone showed up to work without clothes on or didn't show up at all because they didn't turn the key on in their ignition to get the car moving. That's not necessarily to say a person should be fired immediately, but the reaction should be shocked confusion. This is not a hand-in-the-cookie-jar moment; this is more of a finger-in-the-power-outlet moment. You didn't catch them doing something naughty; you caught them doing something unacceptable that makes you concerned for their physical and mental well-being. Thus, you'd be determined to get to the bottom of the situation with them and ensure they understood the behavior was intolerable. Like all corporate cultures, it starts at the top and goes throughout the organization. If you want a safer company, which has countless human and financial benefits, start with creating a culture of safety rooted in how you think about it in the first place.

Constructing Relationships

Building things requires teamwork. Nobody can execute a construction project on their own. Construction calls for groups of people working together on each phase: designing, planning, managing, and building. Companies that understand the importance of their people, the people they're building with, and those they're building for will always outperform those who don't. Get comfortable with the idea of putting people first, and you'll reap the benefits of a more engaged workforce that is more productive, loyal, safe, happy, and profitable. WBCCs are always run with a people-first mindset, without exception. Here's how they do it.

Happy internal and external customers make the company more profitable.

HAPPY CUSTOMERS
- treat us well
- pay what we're worth
- say great things about us in the market

HAPPY EMPLOYEES
- work hard and effectively
- take great care of customers
- say great things about us in the market

Drives Consistently Better GP.
We're paid more for being better and our people take better care of the business.

Reinvest to improve the customer experience.

Reinvest to improve the employee experience.

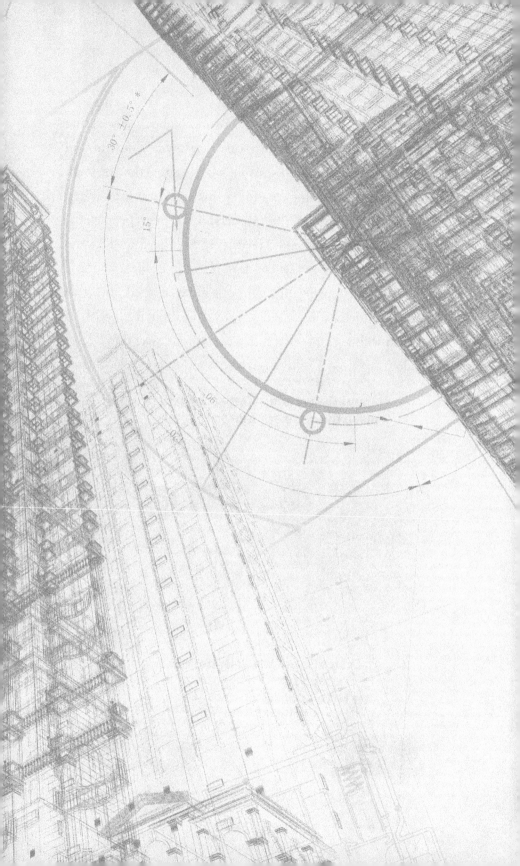

CHAPTER 12

Vendors versus Partners

When it comes to hiring a company to provide a service for you, what is the difference between hiring a vendor versus a partner? Most people think about this in terms of how the customer views the service provider. While this is true, so is the reverse of that statement: how the service provider views the customer. It's a two-way street. Implied in the term *partnership* is a sense of mutual respect and a give-and-take mentality. Something terrible has happened in the building industry, however, in which service providers have grown deeply resentful of customers who don't treat them fairly *and* customers deeply mistrust service providers that seem predatory and misleading. Negative perceptions of *the other* take root, and even new relationships begin with tainted negative expectations. The relationships between customers and service providers in the building industry have crossed the line into fully dysfunctional and have been that way for decades. At the time of my writing, in 2023, the dysfunction may be as deep as it's ever been.

Like any dysfunctional relationship needing mending, both parties must be willing to own up to their responsibility in causing the problem. If we point the finger at the other party, they will continue to point right back. Let's look at ourselves in the mirror and honestly assess what's happening here. Obviously, this is one person's perspective (mine), but it is an outside perspective provided by someone with good visibility into every layer of the construction process. I don't have a dog in the fight, so to speak. I will point my finger around on everyone's behalf:

1. Owners, and all those providing the funding behind construction projects, place an outsize emphasis on securing the lowest possible pricing for design and construction from the outset. This obsession permeates every level in the value chain and causes all members of the AEC community to feel undervalued and commoditized. Owners and financiers should instead focus on the final costs (not up-front projected costs) of construction in relation to the end product they want and learn to place their trust in the hands of capable people who demonstrate their trustworthiness. This would frequently lead to more progressive contracting and project delivery methods, and consistently better end products with lower costs. If they did this, the entire value chain would benefit from improved procurement practices, and it would diminish a ton of the resentment that builds from feeling beaten down on costs.

2. Architects and engineers are agreeing to design contracts that don't give them enough time and money to provide the best and most complete design to the construction team. They know this from the start, but rarely bring it up because their competitors will agree to these insufficient terms, and they don't want to risk losing the project up front. They can produce a better end product but aren't given a chance to do so. In addition, no matter how talented the design team

is, their very best work would still present constructability issues in the field. Designers simply do not have the breadth of experience with actually constructing their projects and can't imagine the challenges posed by environments they haven't been responsible for building before. Truly complete design can only occur as a collaboration between designers and constructors, and the majority of projects don't have the benefit of this collaboration.

3. General contractors are keen to give owners what they're asking for, and owners are asking for the best price. Who can blame them? The reality is GCs aren't doing owners any favors by allowing owners to conflate best price with low price. Since they're often forced to compete on pricing to win projects awarded by owners, there's a game of chicken happening among competitive GCs that are all pretending their super-low subcontractor pricing is correct to present that low pricing to the owner and win the work. Upon winning the work, often the harder job begins ... how the hell to actually build the project with the inaccurately low pricing they've received. Inevitably, this translates into change order battles with owners to get the project to make sense for the GC financially again and keep from putting the low subcontractors out of business. There's an art to doing this without destroying owner relationships, but most GCs haven't mastered it, and this poor practice only exacerbates the lack of trust between owners and GCs that starts the low-bid loop to begin with!

4. More than any other construction factor, the project cost hinges on the combination of all the subcontractor prices. Subs are supposed to be the experts in their individual trades

and scopes of work. Due to the predominance of design-bid-build project delivery referenced above, their expertise tells them that what has been designed in the plans often cannot be constructed as such. They are now met with a very difficult choice: Do they bid the plans as they are, knowing there are constructability issues? Do they communicate problems with the plans and provide recommended scope changes and risk those changes making them look high and rule them out? Or do they go the other way and underbid the project, knowing that significant change orders will be inevitable on the project and will allow them to make back their profit after they've already been awarded the project? Too often, subcontractors have learned that the final option will make them the most money. The resulting risk of disillusionment from the GC, owner, and design team is often not enough of a disincentive for the subcontractors who have learned that they can explain it away and win the next one with the same lowball tactics.

Everyone is frustrated with the next stakeholder ... and with good reason. It doesn't have to be this way. Like all things that make no sense, the industry will eventually move away from this self-defeating norm. If each member of this value chain owns up to their end of the dysfunction and commits to a higher level of honesty and transparency, the entire industry will rise. The scope of this book, however, is limited to sharing the principles I've witnessed in action with WBCCs. There are things you can and should do as a company today to rise above the current dysfunction and engage in better business practices than the norms. This will allow your business to experience a different kind of construction industry in which your added value is recognized and rewarded.

CHAPTER 13

There Is a Customer, and They *Do* Come First

Whatever the contracting and project delivery method, it's vital to maintain awareness that there is someone paying the bills who deserves to be treated like you would want to be treated as a customer. I believe they expect:

1. Honesty and integrity

2. Good communication

3. Follow-through on promises made

4. A kind and courteous experience with their service provider

5. An end product that matches the expectations set at the time of hiring

As a service provider, any variation from these five standards often will, and frankly should, land you in hot water with your customer. Attempts to explain away poor performance on these five standards do not make your construction company better. Instead, they erode your reputation in the market and your internal team culture. You must take full ownership for setting a high standard in your construction company in each of these five categories.

WBCCs have clearly articulated their customer experience standards to every employee, so there is no confusion about what great customer service looks like. It is not enough to tell employees what is expected. Ensuring strong team performance in any arena you consider critical to your business's success must incorporate a comprehensive approach to training and measuring the standard.

Setting the Standard

We've probably all experienced the difference in customer service from one company to another. One example I reference is the difference in fast food experiences from Chick-fil-A to everyone else. Simple touches make all the difference there, don't they? Tastes in food are subjective, and you may not prefer their product to a Big Mac, but how could you not prefer "It's my pleasure" to gum chewing? That extra mile in customer service pays off for companies across all industries, including construction, and the differences are small but meaningful.

Think about every interaction your company has with your customer. From the first time you meet, perhaps at a networking event, to the daily discussions between your on-site management and everything in between. How do you hope your people conduct themselves, and how do you want your customer to feel along the way? Break down each of those potential interactions and put yourself in your customers' shoes. Aim to surpass expectations, not only meet them. Consider things like the preparation that goes into the interaction, and the tone and quality of communication. Consider also what mode of communication is used for the interaction. Will your team make a phone call or send an email when certain circumstances arise? Your standards for customer service should match your company culture so they're natural for your team as well. Build something like the following for each interaction and you'll build a world-class customer service experience, which will translate into better treatment from your customers.

Interaction: Postproject review meeting

Mode of communication: In-person meeting

Your standards:

1. Set this meeting with the entire customer project team to occur no more than one month after project completion.

2. Offer to come to the customer's office or the project location for the meeting.

3. Set the meeting over breakfast or coffee, tell them you will bring food, and bring enough food for more than the team.

4. Meeting agenda:

   □ Prepare and share a list of things you appreciated about your customer during the project.

   □ Prepare and share a list of things you wish you had done better.

   □ Prepare and share a list of things you'd like the customer to have done better.

5. Maintain a constant tone of appreciation for the business, no matter how badly the project went.

6. Always thank the customer for their feedback, even when you disagree.

7. Convey your desire to improve on every project, even when they have only positive feedback.

8. Compile everyone's feedback and send it to the team afterward in a PDF document with the project name and date of the review meeting in the title.

9. Send to the president of your company, who will make a personal phone call to the head of their project team to thank them for the feedback and restate your commitments for improvement.

Training the Standard

Like all process training, your customer service training should recognize that adults don't accept information at face value and immediately change their behavior. Instead, great training programs allow space for participants to challenge the ideas they're presented with. You're engaging their critical thinking by providing training participants the opportunity to voice their opinions and disagree with the instruction. When people feel heard, they're much more open to listening, and training programs have the desired impact, which is changing behavior. Another important element for training success is allowing participants to practice what they're learning.

Creating role-play scenarios to reenact potential customer interactions, for example, may feel awkward. Still, this practice is crucial for team members so that they've spoken the words they need to speak in a similar, albeit contrived, interaction.

Measuring the Standard

- Are we winning repeat business?

- Using a customer survey, how do our customers say we stack up?

- Are we receiving negative or positive feedback throughout our projects?

These are important measures of success you should put in place, but they're lagging indicators. Knowing this information today doesn't impact whether our customers are happy right now. Leading indicators ensure your future health. This sounds great in concept, but how do we measure whether our team is being honest and acting with integrity, for example?

Often this is the type of thing you really need to see with your own eyes to measure. One way to track these types of leading indicators, which are very difficult to track using ordinary tracking methods, is the manager ride-along. Done correctly, this is far from micromanaging, in which a manager dictates to a subordinate what must be done, how it must be done, and when it must be done to a level of detail that removes an individual's sense of agency. Instead, the intent of a manager ride-along is for a manager to watch their team in action under the real circumstances required by their job. Here, you'd be focused on the customer interactions, but these concepts also apply to other measurables. The manager should not dictate how they want the employee to do their job but allow the employee to operate as normal and use their observations to provide feedback and coaching to the employee. Ride-along management should be done with all team members periodically and more often with newer employees, as managers ensure they're performing their roles at an acceptable level early on.

Two-Way Street

To hit the five standards as a service provider, it sure helps to have a customer that treats you like a partner rather than a vendor. It's hard to be honest when your customer becomes enraged with the truth and threatens you. Maintaining good communication is a challenge when your customer doesn't reciprocate by answering your calls and emails promptly or at all. On a construction project, you can only follow through on your promises if the customer and service providers around you follow through on theirs. Some people find it very difficult to be kind when they're under pressure and feeling underappreciated. The end product can sometimes represent the best you could do with the challenges that came your way. As we've said before, it's a two-way street.

Each entity—the customer and the service provider—is responsible for educating each other on (1) what they expect the other to provide, and (2) what they need from the other to meet those expectations. It is reasonable to expect your customer to uphold their end of the bargain, but if you remain committed to delivering an outstanding customer experience, you won't allow the customer to undermine the success of your work together. It is good to always hold up your end of the deal, but it is spectacular when you're prepared to make sure your customer holds up theirs. The thing that separates WBCCs from the pack is that they make it their responsibility to help their customer hold up their end of the bargain. They do this through proactive communication with the customer, ensuring they know what is needed from them and when. They set a lot of small deadlines along the way, and they follow up on those deadlines, which keeps things from getting too far gone. And they are even prepared to step in and work alongside their customers to help them hold up their end of the bargain if they're struggling to get it right.

CHAPTER 14

Always Prepare for Succession

Now let's turn to the internal customer experience.

When most people think about succession, they imagine the often complicated and sometimes contentious issue of passing ownership down to the next generation of a family business. That version of succession is extremely important to most construction companies, which are privately and family owned. In addition to the legal transition of ownership, however, succession can also refer to the transition of responsibilities from those in key roles to new people. Succession in key roles is needed because of retirement, promotions, and other planned or unplanned employee departures. Industry experts have reported that the construction industry's average retirement age is sixty-one, and over one in five construction workers are currently older than fifty-five.[5] If you stop and think about it, the need to

---

5   https://www.abc.org/News-Media/News-Releases/
     abc-construction-industry-faces-workforce-shortage-of-650-000-in-2022

prepare employees to step into key roles is ever present. We'll call this type of succession *positional succession*.

WBCCs understand the importance of positional succession and prepare accordingly. If you're like most, your construction company depends heavily on a select number of key employees to run the business—whether it's the genius behind your estimating efforts, an operations guru with the ability to overcome any management challenge, field employees with incredible experience and problem-solving skills, or the owner of the company who knows of every aspect of the business and is involved in everything. Take a moment now to think through the people in your company that you'd be hard-pressed to live without. Chances are these people are special in some way. You're lucky to have them, and you should take important steps to secure their long-term futures with your company. Far too many construction companies have undervalued top team members, only to have them leave huge holes behind when they seek greener pastures. With that said, as much as you should take steps to keep your key people, prepare for their inevitable departures, and seek to reduce your reliance on a short list of people for the overall success of your business. As we've shown, there are many reasons employees move on from their roles, some planned and others unplanned. Your ability to swiftly backfill those key roles has a great bearing on the business you run.

How often have you seen companies keep people who damage the company's culture just because they're capable of performing in the role and there's nobody else to fill in? The damage these capable but cancerous employees can do to the employee and customer bases is hard to measure but outstrips the damage that would be done if owners had ripped off the Band-Aid and fired them. The fear of what would happen to their business and to them personally if they fired those negative employees keeps owners and executives of construction companies from making these moves. If, however, there are strong and capable employees ready to step into key roles with little to no interruption, difficult but necessary employee changes can be made with confidence for the good of the overall enterprise. WBCCs are committed to building an internal pipeline of qualified successors to all key roles, so they're never forced to accept the unacceptable from their employees.

Another benefit of having key-role succession plans in place throughout your construction company is the flexibility it offers. Most construction companies ignore an incredible number of opportunities for growth because they don't think they can handle it. Many have even programmed themselves so well to ignore those opportunities that they don't even recognize opportunity when it knocks. That great customer who mentioned opening a new office in a new geographic location; the big, complex project you were invited to bid; and the article you just read about a booming new market sector that's underserved … all these things and more are not pursued out of a certain resignation to current limitations posed by a lack of ability to backfill key roles to pursue new potential. You're already too busy, and there's just nobody available to lead these efforts. Meanwhile, a small percentage (here's that 2 percent number again) of your competitors have succession for their key roles all dialed in, and they're free to pursue what you will not. They reap the rewards while you roll with the ups and downs of the same old, same old.

Developing strong positional succession isn't about reducing the importance and value your current key team members have to your company; instead, it's about creating more people with the strengths of your top performers, which, as we have shown, has enormous benefits. For a moment, think about your business like a professional sports team and you as the owner, general manager, and coach. Your team must deliver results to win. To be in the best position to deliver results, you simply cannot risk having no coverage if your star players go down. So you draft potential replacements for your stars, which doesn't diminish the importance of the stars to your team, but it mitigates the catastrophic risk associated with their injuries or departures. If the people playing the backup roles to your stars develop into stars themselves, all the better for your team! We'll stop the sports analogy here, however, because there can be only one quarterback for a football team, while in your business, if a new star quarterback emerges, you can create a new team in a new location with that quarterback. Again, unlike sports, age in business equates to experience, and there is no need to replace employees because they're not young anymore … you get to keep them for as long as you're both getting mutual value! The point is you have a responsibility to keep winning in mind as you build and maintain your company, and a critical factor for your success is the extent to which you have both strong players in key roles today and strong players in development for those roles.

A Culture of Growth

Once you get your succession engine in place and are constantly grooming employees for the next levels in their careers, you must provide them with ample opportunity for growth. Perhaps a fear of growth is the invisible force that keeps many construction companies from strengthening their succession plans for key roles. I've met many construction executives with a healthy fear of growing too fast. There is overwhelming evidence that the biggest risk facing construction companies isn't dying from starvation (not winning enough work), but it is instead dying from gluttony (becoming incapable of fulfilling their contractual obligations). Still, there is another risk worth fearing as much as taking on too much work: the risk of being a mediocre construction company for the long haul. Much earlier, I offered a disclaimer that only companies committed to being better and embracing change should continue reading. This is a gut-check moment for many of you. Is your desire to be a great company greater than your fear of growth?

I want to share a story with you about a person I know who owns a subcontracting company in the mid-Atlantic. He and I met for breakfast to talk about life and business six years back, which we'd do a few times a year. His business was thriving, the market was healthy, and he was in great spirits. He told me he had things "right where he wanted them" and wanted to stay this same size forever. I was happy for my friend, and we spent fifteen to twenty minutes of our time together entertaining this positivity and allowing time to bask in the fruits of his labor. We spoke of his new vacation home, the increased financial security for his family, and the travel plans he and his wife had ahead. The next thing we dug into was my question, "To what do you attribute your great success?" He took no time to answer, "I have three amazing people running our three key departments." He explained the strong veteran talent he had running operations, estimating, and the field. I knew he'd accomplished something that many business owners in all industries dream of: an organization that could effectively operate without the owner's involvement. As our conversation continued, I risked screwing up the positive vibe by asking him about the succession plans behind his three veteran leaders. This changed his facial expression altogether as he fought off the stressful thoughts associated with my question. He didn't want to discuss it, and I could see that. I let it go that morning, but the next time we were together, he told me he had put together a plan for succession for himself and his three key leaders.

He identified two high-potential employees who could be groomed for two of the three positions. That was a good start! If he were being honest, he said, they were more capable than the three key leaders in place. Even better! Because of thinking through succession, he planned to approach the two high-potential employees to share his vision for their future in one of the three key leadership roles. While they were both very grateful to be considered high potential, to the owner's surprise and disappointment, they both had bigger dreams for themselves than filling those roles. They both had planned one day soon to start their own business together. They said, however, that given the opportunity to start a new branch office for their current employer and a path to earning equity in the business, they'd gladly stay for the rest of their careers. This posed a serious quandary for my friend. Remember, he had things right where he wanted them! He didn't want to grow his business beyond where it was right then. Why mess up a good thing?

My friend was unwilling to entertain growing his business, let alone adding branch offices! He wouldn't allow his employees' goals to influence his own fixed vision for his company. He made it clear there would be no such opportunity for them in the business and tried to pitch them on how great it would be if they'd just stick around for ten to fifteen years and take over one of those top three roles. The two high-potential employees left about four years ago and started their own competitive business. Sadly, one of the top three leaders developed cancer and retired early about three years ago. My friend, the business owner, has been completely pulled back into the business. He is neck-deep in the day-to-day and has tried to hire his way out of his problems twice by looking for a veteran to step in. He's paid big salaries and missed the mark each time. His most likely path is selling the business to get his lifestyle back. This is a far cry from where things were just six short years ago. I feel for my friend, but I could see this outcome on the horizon when he set his mind against growth and creating opportunities for his employees to advance and build something bigger with him.

How would you react to hearing the entrepreneurial goals of your employees? Would it excite you, or would you view it as a threat to your equilibrium? While I believe it would be unwise to jump headlong into any growth scheme presented to you, it would be equally unwise to reject growth out of hand because you like things the way they are. In the words of the great University of Michigan football coach Bo Schembechler, "Every day you either get better or you get worse. You never stay the same."[6] So staying just where you are as a construction company, however tempting it may be, is a recipe for eventual disaster. With this, I am not saying you must want to be the largest company of your type or have some aim to double every five years, though both are valid goals. My point is that you must strive for improvement and growth, whatever that means to you, and you must never block opportunities out of some desire to maintain the status quo. If my friend had engaged his two high-potential employees and enabled the kind of growth they had in mind, he would likely have kept them, and one of them could have been there to step into one of those key leadership roles when the unexpected happened to one of his top three leaders in the form of cancer. The owner's time would have remained free, and he could have used it to properly recruit and train a long-term replacement for the key role, allowing the high-potential employee to return to his dream of building a new

---

6   "13 Quotes by Bo Schembechler," Elevate Society, September 11, 2023, https://elevatesociety.com/quotes-by-bo-schembechler/.

branch. Instead, he took several steps backward because he wanted to stay right where he was.

Are you striving for improvement or fighting to stay exactly where you are? Chances are that if you're reading this book, you're in a growth mindset, but beware of the complacency that often goes along with success as you apply the things you're learning herein. In a few years of conscious effort applying the principles you've read here, you may find yourself in a great position you never thought possible. I sincerely hope that for you. I also hope that you will have the presence of mind not to plateau and stop working on your business. Remember, every day, you either improve or you get worse. You never stay the same.

Strong Mentoring

Webster defines mentoring as "the influence, guidance, or direction given by a mentor," and it defines a mentor as "a trusted counselor or guide."[7] Compared to the structured environment of training, mentoring is quite different. We talked about the importance of training in earlier chapters, so I won't belabor the point further here, but as we explore the importance of mentoring, don't let yourself believe that you can have an employee development plan consisting of mentoring without training, or you'll fail to achieve the consistency that comes with great training programs.

Mentoring is happening in your organization all the time, whether you like it or not. Your employees are taking their lead explicitly from the direction provided by those in leadership roles and implicitly by the actions of those around them. The extent to which those individuals are viewed as trusted counselors or guides will determine how they

---

7   "Mentoring," Merriam-Webster, accessed February 06, 2024, https://www.merriam-webster.com/dictionary/mentoring.

model that behavior and listen to that direction. Your organization will demonstrate the behaviors of your most influential employees, not necessarily your best ones. To help mentoring be more intentionally designed to replicate the best employee behaviors, WBCCs often have a formal mentoring program consisting of a team of designated mentors selected because they are the kind of people they'd like to replicate on their team. In this way, the best employees are positioned to be highly influential.

Without overcomplicating it, a mentoring program provides your employees with experiences that enhance their performance in their roles and enrich their lives. The mentor should not be the employee's direct supervisor. They should, however, be more experienced with the company, industry, or role. Mentors provide a more informal channel for employees to talk about their experiences. Conversations between mentors and mentees run the gamut between personal and professional, often leading to valuable relationships for both. Because of being in a position of guiding and influencing others, mentors will often elevate their own performance to become better role models for their mentees. Interestingly, the advice they provide can be the very advice they need themselves, and they improve. Mentees benefit from someone who is not their boss sharing their views and experiences with them. Outside of any supervisory structure, when the mentor provides the same guidance as the boss, the mentee often views that advice as more trustworthy and reliable. I am a proponent of structured mentoring programs. However, a company doesn't need to have anything formal in place to have strong mentoring.

More than anything, you need strong and willing mentors to have strong mentoring within your organization. A strong mentor will not only be a good representation of an all-around performance in their role, but they'll also demonstrate the cultural characteristics you wish to perpetuate. Someone who performs their role in an exemplary fashion but has a negative attitude all the time would not be an ideal mentor if they can't change their attitude. The ideal mentor will see it as an honor to play a role in the development of other people. Because mentors must, by definition, be trusted, it is important that their duty lies with the individual they're mentoring and not with the company. While this rarely poses an issue or conflict, sometimes, a mentee may confide in a mentor some potentially damaging impacts on the business. For example, a mentee may share that they're not happy with their compensation. While you hope that the mentor will counsel their mentee to bring that concern to the attention of their supervisor for discussion, the mentor must not break the trust with their mentee.

For more advice from mentors and mentees alike, be sure to join the Morning Huddle Construction Show podcast at www.themorninghuddleconstructionshow.com.

Challenge Your People

Have you ever had the experience of someone leaving your team unexpectedly and then having to fill their role with someone you didn't think was qualified, only to find they stepped up and did a great job? Many companies have experienced this welcome surprise and wondered just how many other people on their team may be capable of more if they were put in the right situation. To be clear, this entire chapter is dedicated to preventing the surprise I described, so I'm in no way advocating the "throw them into the deep end and let them sink or swim" school of people development. I'm merely acknowledging that sometimes when you do throw people in the deep end, they surprise you and swim! So what am I advocating here? I want you to create environments that challenge your people in the same way as the proverbial deep end does but that include safety nets that protect your business from adverse effects. I guess I'm advocating a sort of "throw them into the deep end to see if they can swim, but if they can't, be there to pull them out and save them" approach.

There's a huge difference between planned experiences designed to challenge employees to accelerate growth versus dropping inexperienced and underprepared employees into circumstances in which they must figure it out to survive. In planned challenging experiences, employees recognize they're expected to perform, and they do feel the pressure to do so. However, they don't feel the kind of keep-you-up-at-night stress they might feel if they were truly on their own. While there may be some value in cultivating your employees' survival skills, the potential for negative consequences on your business for putting someone in that type of situation is simply not worth the potential benefits of developing grit in your survivors. Planned exercises should be the goal, and actual emergencies beyond the employee's capacity should be avoided.

The WBCCs I've spent time with are always creating challenges for their employees that test their mettle while making it safe for them to fail by supporting them if or when things go wrong. In this way, employees are stretched to their limits in circumstances that will be the norm in the future if their careers are to advance, but they're given support by more experienced team members who can step in when an employee has reached their breaking point. In the book *The Talent Code*,[8] author Daniel Coyle shows it is not merely practice at a thing

---

[8]   Daniel Coyle, *The Talent Code: Greatness Isn't Born. It's Grown. Here's How.* (New York: Bantam, 2009).

that makes someone great at it, but it is specific, intentional practice designed to push people out of their comfort zones that seems to have the most beneficial impact on their development.

If you apply this science to the workplace, I believe (and have seen evidence to support) we can accelerate employee development dramatically with structured challenges like what I'm describing here. Imagine hiring people with little to no experience and having them operate at the level of ten-year veterans in less than half that time. If the average ten-year veteran doesn't have the intentional practice that leads to the highest level of personal development, it stands to reason that if we can provide profound learning experiences intentionally, we can pack ten years of experience into a much shorter timeline. That is exactly what I've seen with WBCCs. When you meet their impressive teams, it seems like they must hire the best and brightest. And while they do hire well, it is more accurate to say they put potential people into positions to become the best and brightest. The credit for the successful development of employees always lies with the employees who take advantage of the situations they're in to explore their full potential. Some companies don't create many opportunities for employees to develop their potential, while others do. This is within your control, so why wouldn't you do what you can to put your team in a position to shine?

Here are examples of the intentional development I'm talking about that you can put in play for your construction company:

1. Ask employees to take on responsibilities for different roles on projects. For example, have a project manager estimate a project with coaching from a member of the estimating team. Be sure the estimate gets a thorough review from management before it goes out.

2. Deputize someone to play a higher-level role on a project than their current station, but do so with supervision. For example, have a staff estimator play the senior estimator role on a project, and ask them to lead the scope review meetings with the customer.

3. Incentivize employees to do their job plus solve an organizational problem on the side. For example, come to them with a particularly frustrating issue for the business, such as submittals that are always turned in late. Ask them to create a "task force" and create a process to overcome the problem. The employees who can solve these types of organizational problems are going to be your best candidates for future promotions.

Bringing It All Together

A company with positional succession readiness is ready for whatever comes its way and can experience incredible success along the way. To have strong mentoring and excel at challenging your people, that culture of growth must be in place. It's hard to imagine capable and willing mentors happily developing someone underneath them if they fear the possibility of rendering themselves replaceable and playing a role in developing people who could take their jobs. Many of you reading this may have difficulty imagining your employees accepting the challenges and tests that will accelerate their development because they don't seem motivated. How motivated do you expect people to be when they can't picture meaningful achievement in their careers and don't see paths for advancement? The bottom line is without a culture of growth, your people will lack something personal to strive for. To my (admittedly capitalist) way of thinking, without an individual profit motive, you'll never get people on board with taking on more responsibility for themselves or others. You must decide that your business is going somewhere exciting and do a great job communicating the opportunities it creates for your team.

CHAPTER 15

Eliminate Unforced Communication Errors

There are communication issues at the root of most problems in construction companies and on their projects. Communication issues come in so many flavors, which can create explosive situations and long, slow erosions. Communication failures can cause problems ranging from procuring the wrong materials to creating unsafe site conditions. At stake are project schedules, budgets, and the very safety and lives of our people. Yet for all that's at stake, and as obvious as these communication issues are, construction companies invest too little energy in addressing them. Even more maddening to the observer of these communication issues is the recognition that they're so incredibly avoidable! If you were a dedicated third party whose job was to follow around a single employee all the time, you'd find it easy to spot miscommunications, and you'd be able to set things right.

However, it is much harder to spot communication issues when you're directly involved rather than acting as a third party to the situation. Why is it easier for someone else to see the miscommunication when they're not a participant in the communication itself? Two words: Emotional involvement. It doesn't matter who you are; barring a brain abnormality, you're an emotional creature. Emotions, in all their various permutations, can easily obfuscate the messages being sent in various forms of communication. For example, you're in a great mood, which somehow makes it harder to recognize the seriousness of a potential problem someone has tried to communicate to you. Or let's imagine you aren't a big fan of the person you're talking to, which somehow has made it harder to recognize the positive progress they tried to convey.

Here are some forms of communication issues I've seen at play most commonly in the building industry and some solutions you can apply to overcome these issues:

The Simple Misunderstanding

These happen all the time! Often caused by moving too quickly, the simple misunderstanding is easily resolved once spotted. You sent a cryptic email because you were processing your inbox and had limited time to spend doing so. The recipient thought you meant one thing when you intended to say the other, and the simple misunderstanding plays out in front of you. As innocent as this is, the consequences aren't always so minor. "Stock the third floor" when you meant "Stock the second floor" can mean hours, thousands of dollars, and a lot of embarrassment. The best strategies to avoid the simple misunderstanding are twofold.

First, when you're the one sending a message, slow down. Reread what you're typing, think a little longer before you speak, don't hit send right away, and so on. One of the best innovations of the past decade is the delayed send option in email. Before that existed, I probably hit send on two to three emails per day I had to go back and clarify! Now I still hit send too soon, but I have a window of time to cancel sending that message I often use to reread the email and make it clearer.

Second, when you're the recipient, make a habit of telling the sender what you believe their message is intended to say. For example, if you're speaking with someone, say, "Can I tell you what I think you're asking me to do and make sure I have it correctly?" and tell them what you heard. You'll be amazed how often you require corrections by the message sender and will be glad you took the time to get it straight. If you receive an email you're unsure how to translate, email back asking when you can jump on a five-minute call to ask a few questions to ensure you're clear about their message. Even when you're speaking in person or by phone, taking a moment to repeat back what you believe someone is asking of you can save an incredible amount of time and money from being lost to a simple misunderstanding.

Style Clash

Style clashes are evident across all industries and anywhere with groups of people that need to work together. Simply put, people are all wired differently. Some are outspoken and prone to take over conversations, while others are more judicious in their communication and speak only when they have something pressing to say. Some are loud and boisterous, while others speak softly and earnestly. It is natural for each of us to view our personal style as normal and any variation from that style as foreign.

Miscommunications happen regularly, owing to nothing more than a difference of styles and a resulting flawed translation. Your intentions when you communicate do not always translate, depending on the perception others have of your message when you send it.

Have you ever felt like someone took what you said the wrong way? We feel most comfortable with people who share our communication preferences. If we're loud and boisterous, we enjoy being with others who share those characteristics. We can be ourselves and feel understood when we're with people like us. However, as with any team of people, your construction company has a variety of styles housed under one roof, and people must learn to effectively communicate through those differences.

To eliminate style-based miscommunications within your company, the most important thing is to acknowledge your differences and embrace diversity on the team. People should realize there is no right and wrong personality and communication style and that everyone must adjust their style a bit to meet others with different styles halfway. It starts with each member of your team developing a strong self-awareness of their communication style.

- How do others perceive you when you communicate?

- How do people seem to react to your communication style?

- Do you feel like people don't seem to understand your requests and direction?

- What compliments and complaints have you noted over the years from others about your style?

- What other communication styles rub you the wrong way?

Once your team has improved their self-awareness, they can enhance their awareness of others, which will let them learn to adapt their styles situationally to improve the quality of communication. For example, your outspoken foreperson who communicates loudly and seriously may adjust their style for those members of their crew who prefer an easygoing, humor-based approach. Your foreperson may never be a stand-up comedian, but by trying to adjust to their team even a little bit, they will improve the chances that their message, including the desired intentions, is received.

WBCCs include communication and soft skills in their training curriculum. There are several communication training programs to choose from, and I've never come across one without value. I recommend your team learns a common language from one structured program, as there is value in a shared vernacular throughout the organization to foster improved communication. For example, in the DiSC communication model, each letter—D, i, S, and C—represents a certain communication style. If your team has all received this training, individuals can openly address their style differences and positively work together to adapt their styles for one another. Your foreperson might tell their crew, "I'm a D, and I think some of you might be i's, and S's," and the crew will know just what they mean. In addition to enhancing communication, this training is great for comradery and team building.

Wrong-Mode Syndrome

If you started your career in the building industry before 2010, this one will really hit home. Let me preface this section by saying technology has impacted and will continue to impact the building industry in countless positive ways. The gains in efficiency, cost savings, increased safety, and more are piling up by the day, and it's a wonderful thing. As it relates to communication, however, technology may be responsible for more inefficiency and waste than any other communication issue. It's not the fault of the technology itself, which has its applications, but the fault of the user who has not learned of the limitations and drawbacks of the technologies they're using.

Email, for example, is a great tool for sending important documents with a click that would have had to be faxed or dropped off in person in the past. Email is not, however, a great tool for a conversation replacement. The results can be wasteful when people send emails in situations that call for discussions. You can get trapped in a back-and-forth email thread where you're talking past each other, and frustration mounts with every send. You can find yourself feeling furious about a seemingly angry email from a boss or a customer, causing potentially permanent damage to your relationship. And you're buried in a mountain of emails sent to you for the sake of compliance that keeps you from being able to recognize relevant and important communication somewhere in the mountain of emails that don't require your action.

I've found a handful of simple rules for selecting the right mode of communication that I'll pass along here.

1. Use email with these rules:

   □ Sending formal documents that people are expecting.

   □ Recapping phone calls and meetings to maintain an accurate written record of commitments.

   □ To schedule meetings or phone conversations.

   □ For simple, one-to-three-question clarifications that won't require explanation.

2. If you send someone an important email, call them to make sure they know you sent it … they get way too many emails to guarantee yours will be read promptly.

3. If you're about to explain something, pick up the phone.

4. If you're feeling angry or frustrated with the person you need to communicate with, take a moment to collect yourself, and either pick up the phone, or use email to simply schedule time to talk.

5. Meeting in person takes more effort, but it's worth doing if everyone is really present in the meeting:

   ▫ No laptops open or phones in hand during in-person meetings except for the note taker and anyone who must look something up for the good of the meeting.

   ▫ Get together in person when a group is involved … there is too much room for people to hide and start multitasking on conference calls and virtual meetings.

   ▫ Meet in person when a relationship is unraveling, as being in the same room with someone increases the sense of humanity.

6. Use text messages for simple, timely messages that don't need to be on the record. Things like, "I just got to the jobsite; where should I park?" and "Are you free to talk for ten minutes this afternoon?" are great text messages.

   ▫ Text messages should never be over two sentences long. If they are, consider making a phone call.

Learned Mistrust (Withholding)

Pain is an extremely effective teacher. You put your hand on a hot stove once and never forget the lesson it teaches you. While it's helpful to have good lessons etched into our decision-making in circumstances like the hot stove or getting a speeding ticket, other lessons that are less helpful are equally retained when they're combined with painful experiences. For example, imagine an estimator unsure of a detail on the plans going to her supervisor, only to be made to feel stupid for asking. You hope the lesson is "Get more education in your craft," but all too often, the lesson is understandably, "Don't go to anyone for help, or you'll be made to feel terrible." As the estimator learns this lesson to withhold information fearing retribution, project teams working from her estimates will suffer because of avoidable mistakes in estimates that lead to lost time and money.

While withholding information happens internally, like in our example, it is perhaps most rampant between the different entities on a project team. Think of all the things owners withhold from their architects and general contractors and vice versa! All this holding back of information comes from an often-well-earned sense of fear that by sharing the truth with someone outside your own firm, you'll be financially or legally punished for it. The roofing contractor who thinks, "This material won't hold up in this application, but hey ... it was specified!" is hurting the overall project by keeping their mouth shut, but calling it out and including better materials in their bid will cost them the job! The GC who thinks, "There's no way we're going to be able to recover the two months we just lost due to our mistake in the earthwork bid, but we'll just do our best and allow the schedule to be wrong rather than confront it" is losing the trust and faith of the subcontracting community and the owner alike by failing to confront reality, remake their schedule, and take the lumps of potentially accelerating their subs to get back on track.

We could come up with hundreds of examples of real-world scenarios in which withholding information can and does derail the success of projects and companies alike every day. For you to overcome the withholding issue in your company and on your projects, you must create new lessons for those around you that reward transparency, honesty, and the sharing of bad news. One WBCC I know even celebrates mistakes as learning experiences and highlights the most valuable mistakes of the month in their team meetings. Mistake makers are recognized for their courage in calling out their mistakes, and they're positioned as teachers for their colleagues. It is common for someone to receive a round of genuine applause for owning up to something they did incorrectly and sharing how they learned from it. Imagine that! In addition to rewarding transparency, you ramp up the punishment of withholding information, even when the outcome is positive. The message is loud and clear: the only thing that will get you in trouble is hiding information from others.

Project teams can replicate this same culture with a concerted effort, but sadly, it is all too rare for separate companies working on the same project together to embrace the kind of transparency I'm talking about. It has to start at the top, and I've found that owners who set the standard up front that the project team is *one team* and they're a part of it, too, stand a real chance of encouraging true transparency across the team. I hope to dedicate an entire future book to building highly effective project teams, so for now, I'll just encourage you and your company to embrace transparency internally and externally. This level of honesty may cost you money occasionally on your projects, but the relationships you'll forge by being a company of high integrity will far outstrip your losses eventually.

Nurturing Grudges

How many times have you said, "We'll never do business with those guys again!" over the years? If you're like most of the construction companies I've met, the answer is more than once or twice! Now think back as far as you can, and consider that list in your mind for a moment. How many people on that list have you eventually worked with again? Once more, if you're like most of the construction companies I know, there's a percentage of them, if not most, that you're back in business with. In your geographic area and your unique slice of the market, the construction industry is small, and you'll be seeing the same names repeatedly through the years. Nurturing grudges with people in the industry can significantly limit the list of customers and employees you're willing to work with. This often unnecessarily shrinks your potential for no good reason. There will be times that you're forced to work with companies or individuals you are holding a grudge against, and your income and reputation are at risk if you can't work through your feelings and work effectively with them.

Grudges can be formed in many ways in the building industry. There is no shortage of opportunity for conflict! Sometimes there's a big falling-out that leads to sour feelings all around, but more often, I find these grudges are nurtured privately—almost secretly—against an unwitting person or company with little to no idea of the issue.

Whether carried on knowingly or not, these grudges lead to aggressive and unproductive communication that worsens virtually any situation. I can think of dozens of situations in which team members who must work effectively together cannot overcome their personal issues for the good of the project. In addition to having a negative impact on their work product, the people working around a grudge experience diminished productivity and satisfaction as unproductive conflict taints the air around them. You can't afford to let grudges fester.

There are only two ways I've seen WBCCs successfully deal with this problem. The first, and least desirable, option is to separate team members with grudges from having to interface with one another.

Sometimes that's an easier solution when you can make sure these two people don't have to work on a project together again. Other times, that is simply not a viable option. In one situation at a general contractor between a general superintendent and a project executive, for example, it was unrealistic to think these two could be isolated. The disruption that would have resulted from trying to isolate them would have been worse than their constant battling. If they couldn't sort it out—and, unfortunately, they couldn't—one of them would have to go, and, sadly, they did.

The second, more preferred option is to guide your grudge-holding team members to confront their grievances together and resolve the grudge once and for all. This takes a lot more work, but the results are heavily preferred compared to the separate them approach because they are lasting and improve the overall morale of those around them. It has the added benefit of setting an example for others so that the team can overcome differences and work well together. There are wonderful books on the topic of resolving workplace conflict that can help. I recommend *The Five Dysfunctions of a Team*,[9] by Patrick Lencioni, to most construction executives I meet. There are many lessons from his book I won't try to summarize here, but if you don't have time to read another book and you want to get started resolving your conflicts today, the biggest takeaway I had from Lencioni's book was the importance of building empathy between your team members.

Each of us views the world through our own lens. It is through that same lens we view and judge the actions of others. When we understand where others are coming from, we can view their actions with a sense of empathy that often reduces the intense negative judgments we make without that same empathy. Reduce or even

---

9   Patrick Lencioni, *The Five Dysfunctions of a Team: A Leadership Fable* (San Francisco: Jossey-Bass, 2002).

remove the negative judgments, and two people at odds moments before can find common ground and move forward as friends … or at least amiable colleagues.

To illustrate this point, imagine seeing a car speeding down the shoulder while you and the hundreds of cars around you sit in grid-locked traffic. What thoughts and judgments are you making about the person behind the steering wheel of that car? If you're like most people viewing that action, you judge the person driving the speeding car as entitled, rude, careless—even evil—for potentially putting others in danger. And why shouldn't you? We can agree that behavior is not acceptable. However, what if your spouse had just informed you that your neighbor had gone into labor, and you recognized the person driving that car as your neighbor, her husband, trying to get to his wife's side. Does that make the behavior acceptable? Probably not, given the risk involved to himself and others, but does it at least make the behavior understandable? Certainly, it does.

Meanwhile, no one else sitting in traffic has the benefit of that knowledge about your neighbor and his desire to be with his wife and soon-to-be-born child. Horns honk and drivers scream about the entitled jerk driving on the shoulder! We act based on our own view of the world and the things happening to us in the moment. Your neighbor made an understandable, if flawed, decision to drive on the shoulder to be with his wife in her time of need. The drivers made understandable, if flawed, decisions to scream and honk and offer one-fingered gestures to him. Imagine how that scenario may have played out differently if every driver stuck in traffic had the information about your neighbor's predicament and if everyone had the ability to magically communicate with one another at the same time! I'd like to believe that the drivers would have all suggested they take their next opportunity to safely form a path through which your neighbor could move to the front of the line much faster than the pace of the traffic jam but still safely, so as to respect everyone on the road, and that your neighbor would have expressed deep appreciation for the kindness of these strangers while abiding their efforts to help him without risking damage to life or property. Again, that's what I'd like to think! And I have found, as I hope you have, that most people are good and want to do good. For most people, their own negative perception of the world around them drives them to do not-good things.

The late author and speaker Stephen Covey famously said, "We judge ourselves by our intentions and others by their actions" in his book *The 7 Habits of Highly Effective People*.[10] If we seek to understand why people do what they do, we'll usually soften the negative opinions we had about them based purely on their actions, which lets us view them as good people with flaws ... like us. We would do well to assume positive, rather than negative, intent when we see actions we don't like. More often than not, there is a good person on the other side of those actions with their reasons for taking that negative action. If you can seek to understand their reasons, you can often help them to change their actions in the future.

Simple Rules of Communication

I believe we (rightfully) covered a lot of ground in this section. Before moving on from communication, I thought it would be good to summarize the simple rules of communication I see WBCCs put into practice in their companies. Maybe this is something you can print out and share with your company to foster an internal discussion about communication on your team:

---

10   Stephen R. Covey, *The 7 Habits of Highly Effective People* (New York: Simon & Schuster, 1989), 46.

1. Slow down to communicate completely and accurately.

2. Confirm your understanding by repeating back what you think you hear.

3. Remember, people are wired differently than you, so adjust to their style rather than making them come to your style.

4. Instead of typing, consider picking up the phone.

5. Summarize verbal conversations in emails to confirm mutual understanding.

6. Share bad news, mistakes, worries, and problems with the right people, and do so with urgency.

7. Show patience and understanding with people who come to you with bad news, mistakes, worries, and problems ... otherwise, they'll hide those things from you.

8. Never multitask in meetings or conversations, and if you must handle something, ask for a pause to do so.

9. Assume positive intent when someone does something that bothers you, as they're likely not doing what they did to bother you.

10. Resolve conflicts as quickly as you can once you are emotionally in control enough to do so. Don't let your issues with anyone fester.

CHAPTER 16

Hiring Excellence

Hire for Mindset and Role Fit—Train the Rest

Skills and knowledge are easy to train compared to mindset. I've seen countless new hires with great résumés fail out of their roles quickly and spectacularly. When this happens, it causes everyone involved to step back and wonder how it happened. Were they lying on their résumé? How in the world did they have such experience in their past, seem like such a good fit on paper, and end up being an unmitigated disaster of a hire? It just doesn't add up. Looking deeper into many of the hires that made good sense on paper but didn't work out in practice, we see the biggest source of failure is with the employees' mindsets. So much of a person's success or failure in their role comes down to what their beliefs are about themselves, their work environment, the customers and vendors they work with, the industry, and more. Those beliefs translate into behaviors, and those behaviors create outcomes that either do or do not support the company's goals.

When a new hire should theoretically have the ability to do the job but fails to perform, their mindsets aren't driving effective behaviors or results.

Although years of experience should theoretically bring lessons learned and wisdom, there are a lot of veterans whose experience brings little to no value. Just because someone has been doing something for a long time doesn't mean they're any good at it. Just because someone is new at something doesn't mean they're not outstanding at it. Experience is important, but this prevailing thought in the industry that someone needs to be doing something for X timeframe before they have enough experience to move up is perpetuating the talent shortage in the industry.

It is probably true that, in an environment where an electrician is getting on-the-job training through experience alone, they need a good ten years before they're qualified to move up to the next level. However, as we've illustrated, with a highly focused training program designed to get them a ton of experience both in the classroom and in real-world applications, they can get that same experience in a fraction of the time, letting them take on more responsibility and tougher projects much faster. The question isn't how long a person has been doing something but rather how much valuable experience they've had in the time they've been doing something. Arguably the gold standard for military special operators worldwide, the Navy SEALs are prepared for deployment after seven to nine weeks of boot camp, twelve months of SEAL qualification training, and eighteen months of intensive specialized training. That's under three years to be prepared for the most intense and demanding military operations the world offers.

Meanwhile, I've met construction industry veterans who have told me there's just no way for someone to become a high-level chiller technician without twenty-plus years of mechanical experience. That simply cannot be true! It's time to rethink our definition of experience. WBCCs take it upon themselves to deliver training on the skills and knowledge necessary for their people to perform at a high level in a fraction of the time it would take for someone to amass those same skills and knowledge through merely encountering those situations on the job. Being an excellent training organization reduces reliance on finding people with experience to fill key roles. It also allows you to hire the right people, which means you get to focus on their mindset (translating into culture fit) and their role fit (translating into long-term performance).

Watching people fail due to their own bad mindsets is a painful experience because you know they have what it takes to do the job, but some problems in their own minds are standing in the way. In my role as a coach and consultant, I have been asked to work with many of these tragic figures, and I can confidently say that bad mindsets can be fixed, but it sure is a pain in the neck. The issue is that the target must be open to change, which is uncomfortable! A great coach may help someone discover that they need to make a change, but that's the point: it must be something they discover. Once that's done, making the mind shift is easy. I'd estimate the success rate of fixing employees with bad mindsets at about 10 percent without intervention from someone like me and only maybe 25 percent with professional help. If you're hell-bent on making it work, it is possible but reliant on the person truly wanting to do the work to change their mindset.

Instead, doesn't it make so much more sense to make the right mindset a requisite factor in your hiring or promotion processes for any position? For every sad story I have about people with the right experience but wrong mindsets failing, I have at least five success stories of people with thin résumés but great mindsets becoming rock stars. I'll bet you do too. The president of one large subcontractor I know started with the company when he was a teenager working in the field. His mindset was so incredible that his eventual rise to lead the whole company was inevitable. A senior project manager of another midsize general contractor I know started her career in her midtwenties after not attending college as a receptionist for the company. Her mindset demanded ongoing development and challenges be offered to her, and today, in her late thirties, she is leading project teams for $40 million projects, and she is far from done writing her construction business success story.

So why, faced with overwhelming proof that mindset counts for more than any other trait of a successful team member, do we continue to base hiring and promotion decisions so heavily on the résumé? I think it's (1) force of habit—we've just always relied on that piece of paper to tell us whether someone is qualified for the job, and (2) it's difficult to evaluate a candidate's mindset in the interviewing process. For issue number one, I have only one piece of advice: stop it starting now. Just stop. Experience does matter, but not nearly as much as mindset. I agree that certain high-level roles require a baseline level of experience, but anyone over that baseline should be evaluated on mindset as the top priority. For issue 2, the solution is not so simple. You're busy, and it's difficult to call every person applying for a position. My advice is to lean toward contacting as many as you can, and if you can't do it all, outsource some of that effort to others.

"Suited For" and "Capable Of" Are Different Things

When you're suited for the task at hand, you know it. You don't have to talk yourself into the work … you genuinely enjoy it. The effort feels natural, and while it may not always be easy, performing work you're suited for shouldn't take much mental and emotional energy. In his book *The Productivity Project*, Chris Bailey recommends keeping a time and energy journal for two weeks to identify how you're spending your time and how your energy levels fare for fifteen- or thirty-minute increments each day.[11] The idea is geared around finding the best times of day for your energy without any chemical influences (alcohol or caffeine). In doing this experiment, what emerged for me was crystal clear: I have my best energy from 6:00 a.m. to 2:00 p.m. I also noted that I used a ton of energy when I did focus work that required me to work alone on a solitary project for more than one hour. When engaging in any social activities, I emerged from that time with more energy than when I began! Among other takeaways from this project was that I am capable of solitary work but best suited for social interactions. I still have to do solitary work occasionally, and when I do, I'd be wisest to do so first thing in the morning—as I write this, it's 8:57 a.m. However, if all my working time was dedicated to that type of solitary work, I would find my work positively draining.

In the building industry, most people work at least fifty hours per week, and few take off more than two to three weeks per year. That means that for most, roughly half (twenty-five hundred out of six thousand) of their waking hours per year are spent working. With that much time spent at work, it borders on cruelty for someone to do something they're not suited for. If a person isn't well suited for the work they're most engaged in, they will show signs of fatigue, disinterest, distraction, and other unproductive behaviors. Someone suited for estimating can do some business development activity occasionally, but if you need someone doing business development full time,

---

11   Chris Bailey, *The Productivity Project: Accomplishing More by Managing Your Time, Attention, and Energy* (New York: Crown Business, 2016), 67.

it'd be a mistake to ask your estimator, who is capable of it but not suited for it, to move into that role.

That is a recipe for frustration all around.

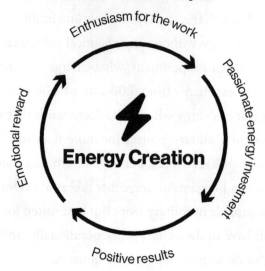

Suited for: Positive Cycle

Enthusiasm for the work

Passionate energy investment

Energy Creation

Positive results

Emotional reward

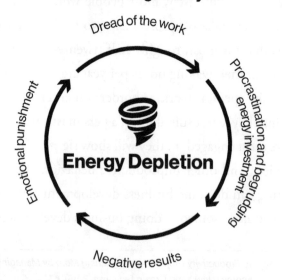

Suited for: Negative Cycle

Dread of the work

Procrastination and begrudging energy investment

Energy Depletion

Negative results

Emotional punishment

Talk to your people about what they enjoy most in their roles. Seek to understand what they are best suited for, and find ways to give them the gift of more time working on things that feel natural for them. People feel less pressure about work-life balance when their work is a source of enjoyment, not just income.

How do I find these people with the right mindsets and role fits?

Assessment Tools and a Strong Interview Process

One way to streamline the evaluation process and uncover more people with the right mindsets who are suited for their roles while reducing your reliance on résumés is to employ assessments as preinterview screening tools. That way, when someone wants to apply for the position, their first step is to complete an online assessment for five, ten, or fifteen minutes (maximum) that will confirm some basic capability for the position. There are plenty of good tools out there. Remember that the goals are to screen for role fit. For example, you may require an assessment for math skills, writing skills, or intelligence level. Real screening tools should evaluate the hard skills and competencies required for the job. Personality tests alone are not good prehire success indicators. They may tell you whether someone is suited for the work, but these assessments are so easy to manipulate that they're not a reliable tool. We use them extensively with existing employees who have much less pressure to sell themselves to the company. It is much harder to manipulate a timed test of intelligence or skill.

Your interview process must also be well designed and consistently followed. My favorite model for interviewing comes from the book *Who*, by Geoff Smart.[12] Their simple but extremely effective model stresses the importance of asking people to thoroughly recount their prior work experience to illustrate how they will perform. It does no good to ask people, "Are you a hard worker?" when anyone with a heartbeat will tell you what you so obviously want to hear. Instead, ask people to tell you what their responsibilities were in their previous roles, how they performed compared to the expectations, their biggest accomplishments in those roles, their biggest failures in those roles, and detailed explanations of why they are no longer employed with previous employers. Repeating this process for all work experience will give you a much clearer picture of the person you're considering. Create an interview scorecard, interview with other people who keep their own scorecards, and make the right hiring decision up front. The extra time interviewing will save countless hours of cleaning things up after making a bad hire.

Market to Candidates

Another thing to be cognizant of is the image your company presents to the potential candidates. Too few construction companies spend any real time, energy, or money on their branding. They think, "I bid for work and win if I'm low. Why do I need to spend on marketing or branding?" What can I say? If you're still carrying around that mindset by this point in the book, please go back to the beginning and read more slowly. We've established that the market players care about your brand identity and the corresponding value they can expect when they work with you. The same rule applies to those who would come to work for your company. Don't try to be all things to all people. You

---

12   Geoff Smart and Randy Street, *Who: The A Method for Hiring* (New York: Ballantine Books, 2008).

don't simply want a high volume of people who might come and try to join your team! You want your kind of people, the kind who will represent the standards you want to see demonstrated daily across your team. It's good for people who don't share your values to see what your company stands for and say, "That's not for me." That approach triggers the people who share your values to say, "Finally, a place for people like me!"

Recruit When You Don't Need To

One of the best things you can do to ensure a consistent stream of the right kind of people is never to stop recruiting for your most populous roles, despite positional openings. Roles like project manager, estimator, foreperson, superintendent, and more are examples of positions your company can never have enough excellent people for. What if you don't have an opening? It's possible, even likely, that you meet people who would raise the bar. If you meet an absolute A player in a position for which you have 50 percent B players today, hire them and figure it out. The worst thing that happens is you let go of lower-quality players to make room. More often, A players expand your capacity to win or perform work, and you don't have to make unwanted cuts. Managers with hiring responsibilities should always meet new candidates who come through your recruiting machine. Imagine regularly meeting four to five new qualified candidates for roles you have no urgent need to fill. Your hiring practices would be careful, you'd have a high standard, and you'd only bring on people you knew were demonstrably the right fit for the job. WBCCs don't wait until there's a need, they don't sweat carrying an extra salary here and there, and they don't hesitate to upgrade the team when the opportunity arises.

Enlist Your Team in Recruiting Efforts

By far, the best source of qualified, right-fit candidates is employee referral. Sourcing people from your employees' friends and family network increases the likelihood of candidate fit from the start because most are known entities. The employee would not have referred this candidate if they didn't consider the person a good fit. Also, the candidate is more likely to take the job because the company is a more known entity from someone they know, like, and trust. While contractors know this source has often proven to deliver great results, they struggle to make it happen. There are a few things you can do to start a successful employee referral program in your business, which we'll cover here. However, the most important factor is the fundamental question of employee satisfaction. Happy employees will refer their network to join your company under the right conditions. Unhappy employees absolutely won't under any conditions. If you finish reading this section and think, "I've tried these ideas, and they didn't work for us!" the problem is your employee satisfaction. Stop trying to get your employees to recruit, and start getting to the bottom of their unhappiness.

Incentive programs are key to employee referral programs. Placing a meaningful reward on the table for employees to bring their network into the company will focus their attention on the opportunity. To determine what is meaningful, ask your employees, but consider paying them at least half as much as you would to a professional recruiter. You're getting a higher quality hire than you would from a recruiter anyway! Being generous with this incentive pays off. Pay a little of the bonus up front, three to six months in, and the balance twelve months in. This way, you are only incentivizing hires that stick.

Setting your employees out to recruit seems easy enough, but most don't know what to say or how to say it. Train them how to be recruiters. Hold a recurring seminar on it with your team and teach them how to approach someone, what to say to gauge interest, and how to close the deal for an interview. With this confidence, your people will follow through.

Building the company's talent base should be part of the job description for executives. Top people in the company should have recruitment as a part of their evaluation and have overall bonuses tied to meeting candidate sourcing requirements, as you might tie bonuses to their ability to achieve a new sales or operating income target.

Diversity

Diversity is a key value of WBCCs. If anything about your culture sends a message to the market that you are not a welcome space for people of different backgrounds or lifestyles, that is not the kind of market presence you want to project. You're looking for people who share common personal values like work ethic, customer service, humility, passion for learning, etc. You should not be looking for a homogenous worldview or similar life experiences. Diversity of thought is a powerful differentiator and a natural outgrowth of building a team with diversity in racial, ethnic, and backgrounds. So while you want your brand image to tell the wrong types of people to look elsewhere, it's important to demonstrate your commitment to hire and retain those who share your values. However, as important as it is, diversity should never cause you to make a hire to fill a quota. You need the right people on your team, period. I'm advocating only that you include a consideration about diversity as a part of that decision criteria.

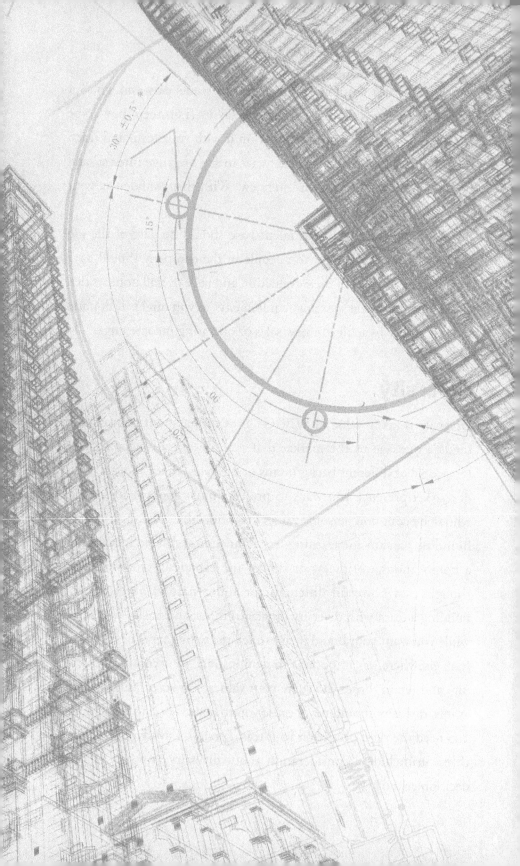

CHAPTER 17

Employee Pride

WBCCs don't just shoot for employee satisfaction; they also want their employees to be proud of where they work. This elevated goal raises the standard from simply meeting your people's needs to inspiring them to think and say great things about where they work. Employees with this mindset are actively engaged in the company's success with every working hour. You don't need to micromanage or police people with pride for their company. They act how you'd want them to when nobody is looking.

Well Built Leaders

Achieving employee pride starts with great leadership. There are many types of great leaders, with no single personality or profile required. Instead, I've watched some leadership principles in action at every WBCC. Here is a list to reference as you think about your company's leadership:

1. Make hard decisions—no dithering.

2. Choose to care personally about all your people.

3. Always seek improvement, both personally and for the business.

4. Encourage people to make their own decisions.

5. Teach people what you need them to know; don't be mad they haven't learned before meeting you.

6. Be principled and act consistent with those principles.

7. Make people feel better when they're around you, not worse.

8. Set goals and do whatever it takes to hit them.

9. Be authentic with your people.

10. Listen closely to what your people are asking for, and don't ignore them.

11. Be willing to get your hands dirty, but don't make a habit of doing other people's jobs for them.

LEADERSHIP MINDSETS

WBCCs promote from within. They groom high-potential people into leadership roles over time. As a rule, they don't hire bosses from outside the company. Preparing people for leadership will require you to train new mindsets. An estimator must have a mindset suited to managing their personal workload, meeting deadlines, and performing highly detailed checks on their work. When that estimator becomes the director of the Estimating Department, their mindset must shift to managing their resources, avoiding a personal estimating workload, and helping the team to master their roles. These are different mindsets, and without the new mindset, the director of estimating will simply be the highest paid estimator on the team, but little more.

How often do we see a great employee promoted into a position they fail to handle? Their experience leading up to this point suggests that they should be ready for the increased responsibility, but once they are in the new position, the things that made them special before seemingly disappear. More than most, the building industry does a poor job of providing employee development programs, let alone training to be prepared for a promotion. In addition to not preparing people for the skills necessary to execute in a new role, companies aren't defining and searching for the right mindsets to perform in a higher-level role. With the wrong mindset, managers will often fall victim to one or more of these traps:

Impostor Syndrome

They felt fear about their ability to perform the role caused by a type of impostor syndrome, a phenomenon occurring in many professionals across industries in which a person feels inadequate despite their obvious qualifications. Their self-identity doesn't let them view themselves as justified in their new role, so they never take full ownership of the duties.

Bad Impersonation

Without ever having any formal preparation for their new responsibility, they do their best impression of the last person they knew who had this role ... who was often not someone who should be emulated. If they worked for a horrible boss in the past, when they become a boss with no preparation for the role, not surprisingly, they act out the only approach they know.

Big-Shot Syndrome

They felt entitled to promotion and didn't show the humility necessary to both learn to perform the role at a high level and earn the respect of others. With this mindset, they have themselves convinced that they're above tasks and they're above others, which leads to resentment from the people they need to perform around them. Failed employees under you equates to failed management. Interesting enough, most people afflicted with big-shot syndrome are actually lacking confidence and have adopted a facade to cover up their own perceived shortcomings.

Gather and Appreciate One Another

Far too few contractors pull their people together with any regularity to enjoy one another's company. People who know and like each other work better together and form bonds that strengthen affinity for the organization. It's difficult to get everyone together, and some may choose not to participate, but create ample opportunities for your employees and even their families to spend time as friends. Do a day at the ball game with employees and their families. Hold a company picnic, and make it fun for all ages. Go to happy hour together and have a little fun. One gold standard is having the office staff visit jobsites every month and having a big team lunch after a tour. You are building awesome stuff! Get out there and make sure everyone soaks that in. Celebrate birthdays, work anniversaries, weddings, new homes, babies, and professional achievement. I strongly recommend creating a company newsletter at least quarterly to recognize the above.

Give Ample Feedback

Everyone wants to know how their boss feels about their performance. With no structured feedback, people are left to form their own impressions based on snippets of interactions. They may feel accomplished in their role and have an inflated sense of value. Worse is that they may only have the vague sense you don't think they're performing well, with no way of knowing what they must improve. While there is no set formula for employee reviews employed by WBCCs, the common thread is that they have a model in place for giving and receiving employee feedback.

Think of a structured feedback system that works for you. I am a huge proponent of monthly one-on-one meetings between managers and their direct reports. That can become overwhelming if the number of direct reports is over five to ten, but it's a good target to shoot for. The process is simple:

- Review action items from last month's one-on-one.

- The manager does a check-in with their employee first.

- How are they? Are they enjoying their work? Is there anything the company can do to help them be more happy or successful? How can I, as your manager, improve?

- Then there is an employee assessment part. This starts with a self-reflection.

    - How do you think you're doing? What could you be doing better?

- Follow this with manager feedback.

- ▫ Here's what I'm seeing as your strengths and weaknesses. This is what I'd love to see you improve in the month ahead.
- • Review action items to check in on next month.

This same model can be done six times, four times, two times, or even once per year instead of twelve, but the higher the frequency of feedback, the more opportunities to build employee pride. The employees improve their performance and gain confidence along the way too.

Release the Wrong People Quickly

It might sound strange, but you build employee pride when you fire the wrong people. You should improve your hiring practices to bring on fewer of the wrong people, but hiring mistakes will still happen. Your team can see they are the wrong people, and good people can't stand having to pick up their slack. Your good people hate the idea that the wrong people might get paid the same or even more than them, and it builds resentment toward the company. Do not force good people to work around the wrong people for any longer than you must. If you have people on your team whom you and others are complaining about regularly today, either fix them or bite the bullet and move them out of the business. I'm all for giving people a shot and doing everything in your power to train and mentor them up to the standard you need, but when you know it is not working, move on immediately.

Compensation Strategy

Linked closely with employee pride, compensation strategy is another critical part to excelling with humans. If someone is going to feel pride about where they work, there's a lot more to it than their income. However, they'd better feel good about their income as well. Compensation strategy is another venue where WBCCs have different approaches, but I've done my best to consolidate common threads.

NO PAYING PEOPLE OFF

You don't have to pay people salaries at the very top of the market. As a WBCC, you have a ton to offer your employees, and you don't need to pay all employees more than they'd make anywhere else to happily stay with your company. Your compensation plan should be well researched and competitively positioned in the market, so you're at least in the high-average range for compensation. If you don't know where to start, there are various tools to do salary research in your market online, such as glassdoor.com.

If you are underpaying someone, go to them proactively and tell them you're giving them more money because they're worth it, and you want to be sure they're getting a fair deal. Don't withhold that information. When they find out, they'll take off, which will hurt your company more than a few more bucks a month in salary. If you find you are underpaying many people, tell them that you're aware of it and working on a timeline for bringing their incomes up to a market-competitive level. They'll appreciate your candor, and their loyalty will increase. If someone you wish to keep tells you they are leaving for more money, only match their offer if it is within the bounds of the pay brackets you establish for that position or if they are ready for a promotion. Paying people more than your established pay brackets just because they threaten to leave sets a dangerous precedent. If your processes and culture are strong, they are replaceable with minimal pain.

COMPENSATION TRANSPARENCY

I mentioned pay brackets in the section above. This means that for every position in your company, you should establish brackets for the compensation range. This information should be publicly available to your team. People on the low end of the pay bracket should want to earn their way to the top. People at the top know that their path to more income is through increased responsibility associated with promotions. It can be scary to implement initially, but in my experience, and probably yours, employees can and will discuss what they're getting paid, despite what the handbook may say. The best policy is compensation transparency.

EFFECTIVE BONUSES

Years ago, the owner of a midsize specialty contractor spoke with me around the holidays, and he sounded down. I heard the tone in his voice and asked what the matter was. He said something that has stuck with me since. He said, "I just paid over a million dollars in bonuses that I don't have to pay just to make my employees upset that they didn't get more. I hate this time of year. I give away my money to feel depressed." This rings true for so many construction company owners who do the same old annual bonus based on leadership's subjective views of your contribution and company profit, which is a secret number. No wonder people are disappointed in their bonuses in such an opaque system where they feel no control. Bonuses can be a fantastic way to incentivize team performance, or they can be an annual tax paid by owners to prevent people from quitting with questionable effectiveness. WBCCs are using bonuses effectively. They do so by following rules, which I will share with you below:

- Link bonuses to above-average performance.

  □ You don't pay bonuses for normal performance. That's what salaries and hourly wages are for. Bonuses are for recognizing people for above-average performances only.

- Team bonuses with individual subjectivity.

  □ Construction is a team sport, so all must be considered when the team wins.

However, your top performers should earn more than middle performers, and the team is allowed to know that. The kicker doesn't expect to be paid the same bonus as the quarterback for winning the Super Bowl.

- Pay bonuses as frequently as possible, and stop paying holiday bonuses altogether.

  □ Quarterly is good; monthly is better. Even look for ways to give bonuses as often as daily if possible. Amazingly, receiving $50 in cash on a Friday for a great week's work is more memorable than $2,000 minus taxes at the end of the year.

- Minimize commissions. It incentivizes the get-work team to think of themselves as outside the broader system of building successful projects. You only win work because the whole team does a great job ... not just your salespeople, business developers, or estimators.

- Commissions can incentivize aggressive salespeople to grow your business, so if that's a fit for your culture, just ensure commissions are not paid on projects until they've been profitably completed.

- Instead of commissions, consider including the get-work team in the overall bonus pool for profitable projects like everyone else.

  » Perhaps they can enjoy an immediate award bonus when you're awarded a project, but that should be a relatively small amount compared to their total bonus potential.

- Incentivize more than making money.

  - A bonus system that fails to account for safety, quality, team play, and other cultural requisites will create a mindset of profit over all else. Be sure you incorporate your core values into your bonus model.

  - Use your one-on-one feedback sessions to communicate to a person about their bonus eligibility based on these added criteria.

Powering Up the Building

As discussed earlier, you'll win a share of work in the construction industry just by focusing on operational excellence. It is an account-based and project-based industry, and the people you've delivered results for in the past, your accounts, are likely to hire you again if you continue to deliver.

Being project-based means there is a clear beginning and end to every project and, therefore, a beginning and end to every source of revenue. Being account based means you can do business with or through the same customers or accounts repeatedly. Construction projects, by definition, start and finish, so you must constantly provide your business with enough work to keep everyone busy and pay the bills. Your business is a machine, your people are the parts of the machine, and the machine needs fuel. For most contractors, it's not like you can sell a big project and coast on that for years at a time. You probably require several projects a year to maintain and several more if you want to experience growth.

Although it is important to fuel the machine, so to speak, shockingly, few contractors are intentional about the effort. Instead, contractors' default position is inattention to sales when the company is busy with active projects, followed by a panic to bid everything they can when they need more work. The results are peaks and valleys, which, depending on the size and type of your workforce, are met with corresponding layoffs and furloughs that damage morale and your ability to retain talent. Many contractors don't think of themselves as "selling" anything. Instead, they think of their project pursuits simply as bidding and waiting, with the occasional follow-up to see whether their price looks low enough to win.

If either description feels a little close to home, this section will challenge the way you think about how you pursue construction projects. As hard as this mind shift may be, the approach outlined in this section can potentially change the game for your business. For those who are already strategic and intentional about their sales and marketing approach, this section will be music to your ears, and you'll have no problem incorporating some of these next-level strategies into your business. Let's dive into how you can eliminate your peaks and valleys and win work in a more predictable, profitable way.

Stake Your Claim

With your CSD and your team's positive identity humming, you should be confident enough to tell the outside world just exactly who you are and who you will become as a company. Your target audience should view your construction company as the clear go to for your chosen path.

One company's CSD was to expand their scope to capture nearly double the revenue on every project they pursued. As they sought to tell the market about this change, they had to confront challenges along the way. First, they were a well-established brand in their primary trade, and people didn't think of them as having the additional capabilities they were claiming to provide. Second, customers had existing relationships they were used to providing the additional scopes. Third, they would not be less expensive than their customers' current options, even though they believed they could add more value. It was not a problem getting GCs to allow them to bid on the other scopes ... I mean, what GC doesn't want more sub numbers? So that wasn't an issue, but they had a hard time convincing these GCs they were a capable and viable option. There's nothing like proving it to get people on board, but how do you get the first at-bat?

They changed all their marketing collateral (web presence, presentation materials, and brochures) to reflect their new capabilities. They made press releases about their new capabilities and sent them to their clients and targets. They developed new company messaging about what they do, and the business development team received training to ensure they could deliver that message with impact in the market. They even developed educational content showing their expertise in these new areas, boosting their credibility. Then they did the boldest thing of all: they turned down certain projects with longtime clients unless they were awarded the full scope they were bidding. This resulted in a handful of key breakthroughs that helped them prove their value with these new scopes, and today at least 50 percent of their projects have their full desired scope, and their average project size has tripled over the last ten years since that move.

Breaking down that example, we see four things that jump out as action steps you can take to stake your claim:

1. Develop compelling, customer-centric messaging about your brand identity.

2. Create interesting and valuable content to boost your credibility.

3. Train your team to deliver the brand identity message effectively.

4. Walk the talk by making the hard choices to change your behavior.

Let's dive into a little detail on each step so you can find the practical application steps for your company.

Develop Compelling, Customer-Centric Messaging about Your Brand Identity

You think your company is great, right? If not, choosing your identity will help you find the conviction that your company is different and better than your competition in meaningful ways. If you aren't convinced that your company is great and you aren't clear on your identity, building compelling messaging will be difficult for you, so consider getting that part straight before working on this element.

OK, so let's assume you think your company is great. Here's the thing: your customers really don't care how great you think you are. It's not because they're jerks; it's because they're busy thinking about their own business, their own goals, and their own problems. Your company, as great as you are, isn't on their priority list. We're all faced with a barrage of marketing messages every single day, and most just blend in with our day like white noise in the background. So how can you create messaging that cuts through the noise? Marketing is both an art and a science; there's no shortage of brilliant ideas out there worth running down. Some of my favorite ideas come from a book called *Building a StoryBrand*, by Donald Miller.[13] The idea at the core of his philosophy is that brands must stop putting themselves in the center of the story they present to their customers. Every person views themselves as the hero of their own story, so why would your customer be interested in hearing about some other hero? They've got a world to save on their own! Instead, brands should position their customer as the hero of their own story and position their brand as a guide to help the hero win the day. I'll distill this idea into something simple

---

13   Donald Miller, *Building a StoryBrand: Clarify Your Message So Customers Will Listen* (New York: HarperCollins Leadership, 2017).

for practical application, but I recommend that you read, or at least your marketing team reads, Donald Miller's book.

Instead of listing all the wonderful attributes of your construction company, think of all the wonderful impacts those attributes have for your customer. Then picture what life must be like for your customer, the struggling hero, who isn't enjoying the wonderful attributes you bring to the table because they haven't discovered your solutions. With this picture in mind, put the customer (not your company) at the center of your marketing, and talk about the problems other heroes like your target customer have had, the negative consequences of those problems (lost time, extra costs, unhappy employees or clients, etc.), and how working with your company helps the hero win the day. Examine all your marketing and engineer it so your customer cares by putting them at the center of your messaging.

Create Interesting and Valuable Content to Boost Your Credibility

In addition to adjusting your company marketing to position your customer as the hero, another fantastic way to position your brand as the go-to for your target market is to create interesting and valuable content about your areas of expertise. I'll explain what I mean, but know that this is a mind-boggling concept for some construction companies, and I expect your reaction to be a combination of frustration and confusion at first. Here's the deal: nobody is watching your company history video. They're probably not even checking out the awesome time-lapse footage of your last amazing project, which is a huge mistake because I saw it, and it was awesome. But you know what they will click on? An article titled, "The Three Scope Items No GC Has Coverage On in Their Drywall Bid." That article might get hundreds or even thousands of views if posted on LinkedIn or other social media outlets, shared in an industry publication or your newsletter, and featured on a blog. One two-minute video I posted, "Subcontractors Win More by Lying," was shared dozens of times and viewed over ten thousand times, leading to lots of interesting conversations with my target audience and some actual sales, but most importantly, a boost of credibility. In the eyes of my audience, I understand their challenges. The goal isn't to sell jobs with your marketing material (although it's nice). The goal is to position yourselves as the absolute go-to for your brand identity and leverage that position in the market to own your space.

Train Your Team to Deliver the Brand Identity Message Effectively

With your marketing materials all delivering the same compelling message to the market and value-added content furthering your credibility with your target market, the only thing that can screw it up is your people undoing all that work with unclear or old messaging when they're talking to your customers. One estimator telling the PM of a key GC, "Yeah … we're trying to get into X, but I don't get it," is enough for your positioning to return *to just like all the others* status immediately. Even if the team buys into the brand identity, they'll still need training to deliver the company message effectively to the market. With that said, I don't think training people like robots to repeat the company message verbatim makes sense. The brand identity speaks to different people in different ways, and I strongly prefer providing the team with some structure for delivering the message and letting them put their own spin on it from there. The message must include the key elements you're trying to communicate to the market about your brand identity, and it should be delivered in a customer-centric way.

For example, "We're an electrical contractor performing both base building and remodeling projects for general contractors who build schools, hospitals, and data centers. Our customers cannot afford to hire an electrical contractor who falls behind on the project or makes excuses about coordination with other trades. Our customers build partnerships with their owners and are looking for trade contractors who treat them like partners as well, before, during, and after construction." This message cuts through the noise by focusing on the customer's experience as the top priority. It's not a message about the electrical contractor; it's a message about the general contractor in the context of their experience with electrical contractors. The general contractor is the hero of the story, and their trade contractors who understand partnership are there to help them win the day. It also has clear elements of the kinds of work the electrical contractor wants to do. Give your people great examples of your messaging, and role-play situations in your weekly meetings to confirm the team is spreading your ideal brand identity without unraveling it.

Walk the Talk by Making the Hard Choices to Change Your Behavior

When the rubber meets the road, you'll be tested. Past customers will call and ask you to look at a project that no longer fits your target market. You'll have a slower estimating month, and opportunities that don't fit your sweet spot will come in. Your operations staff will alert you that if you will really become the best at X, you need to invest in people and equipment. These tests are the hardest part for every business I've watched go through this process. Change can be difficult, and adversity will test your resolve. If you stick to the plan, you may endure short-term hardships, but if you deviate from the plan, you will not achieve the change you set out for. Furthermore, if you make excuses and deviate from the plan, you'll undermine all the effort you've put into building the plan in the first place, as your team loses faith in the brand identity they bought into. Companies that have clearly staked their claim in the market and are known as the go-to have had the discipline to stick to the plan. It does mean, however, that your plan must be well built.

CHAPTER 19

Maintain a Healthy Diet

A character in the novel *Those Who Remain*, by author G. Michael Hopf, says, "Hard times create strong men, strong men create good times, good times create weak men, and weak men create hard times."[14] Replace *men* with *construction companies*, and remember that quote as you read this chapter.

As we've shown, the construction industry is an account-based project sale. Construction executives have learned that what this really means is whatever the circumstances for your construction company today, good or bad, they won't last forever. Unlike an industry such as insurance, in which companies must only sell a new client one time, and the rest of their energy goes into keeping them, the nature of a project-based industry consists of finite starts and finishes, constantly focusing on what's coming down the line, with no time to linger on current success. At the end of your current projects, you'll be back at absolute zero if you don't find the next ones, so good construction companies are always looking over the horizon and, as we illustrated

---

14 G. Michael Hopf, *Those Who Remain* (CreateSpace Independent Publishing Platform, 2017), 82.

in the chapter on measuring what matters, tracking their pipelines to ensure their tomorrow will be as bright or brighter than today.

Let's layer into the project-based environment some of the economic realities faced by construction companies as well. International, national, state, and even local economic factors all factor heavily into the environment in which a construction company must operate. It's common for a construction company to have a good financial year as the economy weakens. Most construction companies don't become aware of a weak economy until the realities of it are already upon them, and they're losing money. WBCCs have their eyes on the leading indicators that show how a weakening economy will affect them, which gives them the ability to plan and not be surprised when the bottom drops out. Learning how to weather the ups and downs of one's market is necessary for those seeking to become a WBCC.

Here comes another diet analogy (sorry!) to illustrate the conundrum created by economic ebbs and flows for construction companies. Imagine being in a tight personal financial situation. For me, I have a reference point: college. When you have little ability to buy anything, what kind of food do you buy? Well, that's easy— ramen, right? Right! And when someone down the hall in your dorm has an extra slice of pizza and asks if you want it, you're not asking what's on it; it's a simple "Yes, please" response. When you need to eat to survive, you're not really picky about what you eat. Nor should you be! Your focus should be on survival, not finery. While neither ramen nor leftover pizza is the best health choice for your body, they're better choices than starvation!

Now leftover pizza and packs of ramen are acceptable survival fare, but eating that way over a long stretch will leave you over-weight and sick, owing to your overly processed diet lacking essential nutrients. When your financial situation improves, you'd do well to buy fresh fruits and vegetables and enjoy a healthy, balanced diet for the long haul. It'd be good to learn to say no to that leftover piece of pizza and develop some self-discipline so that you don't overeat. In this way, you'll enjoy a healthy weight and reduce your chances of chronic illness so that you can feel great well into your golden years. Sounds easier than it is, clearly.

In a project-based industry tied so closely to the tides of the economy, construction companies that have been around for at least a decade have all weathered tight times and enjoyed plentiful times. In tight times, they become survivalists and pursue whatever projects exist to make it to another day. However, the difference between an average company and a WBCC can truly be seen in how they handle their business in plentiful times. While most construction companies allow the tight times to create an ongoing sense of desperation for their business, WBCCs recognize the opportunity to optimize their health by establishing parameters for a healthy diet while the market allows it. They know the difference between proverbial ramen and pizza compared to fruits and vegetables, and they choose the healthier options more consistently for the health of their business.

Construction companies with no discipline on the amount and type of work they consume are following a recipe for becoming overwhelmed with too much work, and to compound that problem, the work they've taken on isn't even healthy for their business. This leads to chronic business diseases like hypertension, diabetes, and … wait … I mean, high revenues, low profits, burned-out employees, and angry customers. When this type of unhealthy construction company, barely hanging on by a thread during the plentiful times, meets the next recession, it'll often be the knockout blow that closes their doors for good.

Create a Project Hierarchy

Think of this like a food pyramid for your business at which the base of the pyramid represents the projects that are the healthiest for your business, and the top of the pyramid represents those projects that should be avoided, except on rare occasions like doing someone a favor or when you must become a survivalist. Make sure your leadership, business development, and estimating teams understand your internal project hierarchy, and exert their energy to match. If you're always in pursuit of projects in those categories healthiest for your business, you'll be able to be much more selective in good or even not-so-good times. Be thinking about ideal project scopes, sizes, locations, durations, and more. Be thinking about ideal customer profiles, too, which can factor into whether you say yes or no when a project is a little outside the lines for you.

Example Project Hierarchy
Note: Yours should be unique to you

0% — **Unhealthy Projects:** proven not good for us. *Target: 0%*

20% — **Gap Fillers:** Smaller projects, easy to do. Not exciting for the team, but nice to keep us busy. *Target: 20%*

30% — **Stretch Projects:** Difficult and/or very large; requiring more resources, but good profit if done well. *Target: 30%*

50% — **Healthy Projects:** Projects that are right in your wheelhouse. Your team enjoys the work and performs it confidently. Customers rave about your performance. *Target: 50% of revenue.*

This process should lead to a clear go/no-go criterion you can use as an objective tool for running your estimating department daily. Most construction companies decide what to pursue and what to ignore based on these factors in an informal gut feel kind of way. Interestingly, this method works out most of the time, but when companies take the time to get those rules out of the head of the business owner or chief estimator, they often find key improvements in the logic that they hadn't seen before. By becoming more objective in your go/no-go procedures as a company, you'll be able to communicate rules to employees more effectively, so executives can extract themselves from the daily decision-making that goes into which projects to pursue and which to avoid. Once the go/no-go criteria are in place, the process should be much more expedient and data driven, but you should conduct an executive review at least annually to help ensure you're not letting the system override your good judgment. Every time your good judgment overrules the system, however, the best practice is to adjust the system, so we have less and less subjective, judgment-based interference.

One key consideration for whether to bid the work is when the work is slated to be built. Estimating must remain focused on the pace of estimates and the pace of sales for the time revenue is needed. The estimating function, while it doesn't generate revenue (only sales, which is future revenue), must work from the projections described in earlier chapters to focus on sales projected to become revenue when the team needs revenue and to keep its resources fully occupied.

I've had construction companies tell me, "Chad, this is all great in concept, but those rules go out the window when we need work!" I agree! Sort of. We've established that your economic realities as a business can and should influence your business's willingness to add less ideal business to your menu, right? As you're building out your go/no-go criteria, factor those rule changes and adaptations into the system so that you can give some good, objective thought to how your business should react to economic pressure rather than letting the emotion overcome you. I've seen many companies start panic-bidding everything that comes in when they have a bad economic forecast, and that result is often that they end up taking on way too much unhealthy work at terrible margins and must ride out that mess while their competition remains free to pursue the good work when things recover. Discipline, my friends.

Go for Volume of Relationships, Not Bids and Not Revenue

It is better for a $20 million construction company to do $1 million of work with twenty customers than it is to do all $20 million with a single customer. While this kind of diffused risk is logical and hard to argue against, it proves to be extremely difficult for construction companies to achieve in practice. It's much more comfortable doing as much business as possible with a customer you know than saying no to that customer on some of their work and pursuing more of your ideal work with someone new. The biggest and best argument I've heard against saying "No thanks" to your current customers on projects they want you to pursue is, "I don't want my competition to get a foothold in there!" This is understandable, and I share the desire to be viewed as the only service provider for my customers, but the truth is you're not doing you or your customer the best service by taking on too much of their work if it's unhealthy for your business.

WBCCs leave their customers wanting them more often than they can get them. They operate in their sweet spot and deliver such amazing results that their customers want them to take on more.

These top companies do incrementally take on more, but they do so with restraint. WBCCs want every qualified customer to hire them for their ideal fees on the projects at which they can excel. When times are plentiful, this enables these companies to thrive by doing the healthiest and most profitable work for them, and when the economy tightens up, they are seen as top performers by many more customers than their competition. As a result, they have more friends to rely on to make it through the tough times, and I have seen several of these companies achieve growth when the market was shrinking due to their top reputation and their increased availability. WBCCs almost always grow market share and sometimes even their revenue during recessions for this reason.

Adjust Your Diet Proactively Periodically

You alone cannot decide what kind of projects are available in the market. Let's say you were a design/build MEP that had figured an efficient and spotless design method for data centers in partnership with two great GCs in your geographical market. As the market became flush with data centers, this knowledge provided a fantastic strategic advantage for you on these projects, and you became the absolute go-to for data centers. Then, all the data center business dried up! Well, you'd have a choice to make, and staying the course couldn't be one of them if you hoped to survive as a business. You could explore other geographic areas and become more regional or even national in your focus on data center work. You could branch off into other high-tech buildings that would apply the same knowledge within your geography. You could diversify and explore other market sectors altogether within your geography. These are all potential solutions to the problem, but one thing is crucial: the decision must be made before the market has shut down! So many times, I've seen construction companies with absolutely no established portfolio in an arena scramble to bid that work with almost no chance of winning just because that market segment got hot when their normal sweet spot cooled off. It's a sad spiral of chasing work without a chance to win without being dangerously low, which has devastating effects.

WBCCs are plugged into market trends, paying close attention to relevant publications, speaking about the state of the market with customers, vendors, and competitors. They participate in local and national peer group opportunities and are active in many associations, so their ear is always to the ground. There will always be unforeseen market shifts, as we saw in 2020 with the COVID-19 pandemic, during which you must react and roll with the punches. However, most ebbs and flows in market sectors and geographies are more gradual and can be studied and planned for. Don't get so committed to the diet you've worked hard to establish in this chapter that you fail to recognize the signs that your primary food sources are disappearing.

CHAPTER 20

Deliver, Sell, and Buy Value over Price

The Most Expensive Whiteboard of All Time

Have you ever bought something that was the low-priced option and regretted it? Of course, you have! All of us have found ourselves being penny wise and pound foolish occasionally. The company I worked for in 2010 was evaluating smartboards, which at the time were relatively new technologies to enhance the experiences of attendees of our training sessions. The cutting-edge technology at the time was more than $15,000, while the best-value products were in the $10,000 range. We spent weeks considering options, and when we unveiled the product we'd selected, it was hard to hide the confusion and disappointment from the team when they saw the bottom-of-the-barrel product we had selected. It was a $3,500 model lacking in many of the key features we were all looking forward to using.

Furthermore, even after hours of training on using the technology, none of us felt comfortable with the interface. When we did have the courage to try it in front of a room full of students, inevitably, the technology would fail. We'd be embarrassed, as we would have to restart in the middle of a class. Students made fun of the cheap equipment, and something intended to improve their experience proved to do exactly the opposite. We disconnected it from the computer interface and used it as a whiteboard … the most expensive whiteboard of all time. This situation illustrated an important lesson that, as a sales training company, we had taught our clients many times: the bitterness of poor quality will remain long after the sweetness of low price wears off. What was so poignant about this situation is that we did not practice what we preached, and it sent a confusing cultural message to the team and our clients. Were we about the best value or not?

Finding the Sweet Spot

When we put price ahead of value, we often get this kind of letdown. You know this, and hopefully, your aim is not to be the low-cost provider in your market because such a path will inevitably lead you to have a reputation for letting people down. Choose instead to find the sweet spot in your market that lets you deliver great customer value at a competitive price.

WBCCs are typically in the upper-middle price range of their respective markets. In a competitive bid situation, their price will not be so high that they're not even in the competitive pack, but it will trend higher than the comparably sized competition. That slightly increased price point represents their added value compared to the same. They have learned what qualities (other than price) their ideal customers care about most, and they reliably deliver those things in a manner that is noticeably better than their competition. Higher margins result, providing myriad benefits, including some cushion to pursue target projects more aggressively when necessary.

I've personally seen several companies engage outside experts to survey the market about what customers care about every three years. More than performing a customer satisfaction survey, they're seeking insight into the challenges facing their market to spot opportunities to bring deeper value all the time. Remember that because they have also chosen their identities well, they are not trying to be all things to all people. It's extremely difficult to deliver better value across many market segments, project types, project sizes, and geographies, so WBCCs aim to be the absolute best value within their chosen identities only. This attainable and sustainable aim consistently pays off as slightly higher margins; better hit rates, which translate to a lower cost of sale; better customer loyalty; and admirable reputations, attracting new customers and employees. If the organization stays within itself, this positive cycle perpetuates and can sustain over the long haul through leadership succession and market cycles, insulating the company from downturns.

As a good friend says, "The best painter in town never has to worry about having enough work." That best-painter analogy is worth looking into a little deeper. The most obvious element of the analogy is that the people known as the best at what they do will always be in demand. Underneath that is the idea that the best painter in town can't do it all when there is a ton of work to go around. She has a long waiting list, and even though they wish they could work with the best painter in town, many people will have to work with someone else. When times tighten, however, and there is much less work to go around, the best painter in town is now available. Why would you go to anyone else if you had a choice?

Every market has a sweet spot where WBCCs position themselves as the best value. The sweet spot is defined as the perfect balance of value and price for the target customer in that market. Think of a spectrum on which top quality and service are on one side, and low price is on the other. Now bend that spectrum so it is in the shape of a horseshoe.

In the middle of the horseshoe is the sweet spot, where quality and price are equally balanced, and the target customer sees value and is happiest. Their needs for quality and service are being met well, and their need for a competitive price is met within reason. Even within the sweet spot, there is a spectrum of lower but not insufficient quality combined with a slightly better price, compared to a higher level of quality at a slightly higher price. You must determine where you want to orient yourself within the sweet spot, but I strongly recommend you emulate the WBCCs by identifying the value with the best return on investment in the eyes of your target customer and edging your price toward the top of the sweet spot. You can always negotiate your prices down as needed and remove added value within the limits of the sweet spot, but once you're toward the bottom end of the price spectrum within the sweet spot, there's little room for error before you simply can't afford to provide the value necessary to meet the minimum requirements of the sweet spot.

The customer is unhappy at the top of the horseshoe, where there is a heavy imbalance toward pricing on one side and an equally heavy imbalance toward quality and service on the other. When they discover they paid too much and don't need all the bells and whistles they signed up for, they feel disappointed for failing to conserve their financial resources. When they discover their desire to pay less actually costs them more time, energy, and money than if they had made a higher-value purchasing decision up front, they feel the acute sting of buyer's remorse. Let me repeat that the horseshoe represents only your target customer, and depending on your target market, the horseshoe changes considerably. Don't know what your customer values most? Make it a mission to meet with and interview them until you get a clear picture of the priorities that are most consistent from person to person. Ask, "Other than price, what are the factors that matter most when you consider hiring companies like ours?" Don't assume you know that your customer only cares about schedule, budget, and quality. They do care about those things, but there are unique foci within each target customer type worth digging into specifically. It may be nuanced, but understanding and uniquely catering to the nuances will become your competitive edge. For example, a public school system hiring a GC will focus on a proven track record of meeting aggressive construction schedules in partially occupied spaces, with schools inevitably opening on predetermined dates. Contrast that with an affordable housing developer who may prioritize value-engineering skills and be willing to accept a more lenient window for turning over units.

The Value Spectrum

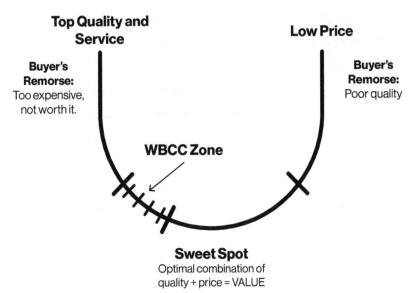

Top Quality and Service

Low Price

Buyer's Remorse:
Too expensive, not worth it.

Buyer's Remorse:
Poor quality

WBCC Zone

Sweet Spot
Optimal combination of quality + price = VALUE

Buy How You Want Your Customers to Buy

A subcontractor spent decades enjoying their position at the upper-middle level of their sweet spot and mastered the art of selling and delivering on that value to the point that they were able to maintain hit rates consistently three times the average of their competition and margins three to five points better on top of it. To expand margins further, for a three-year period, they experimented with more price-driven procurement practices with their vendors and subcontractors. They began more aggressive negotiation in procurement and gave some low-priced providers a shot at their work. For a year, their margins rose, their hit rates stayed the same, and the experiment was widely considered a success … on paper. In practice, their operations and production staff were scrambling to cover the mistakes of their new subs and vendors. Employees were burned out, some quit, and morale was low. The goodwill they had established with their providers was replaced with resentment and an unwillingness to help.

Rapidly, their ability to deliver the value they sold was undermined. By year 3 of this experiment, their hit rates had dropped by 50 percent, and their margins at the time of sale had eroded to the same levels as they had prior to this experiment. They had simply slid to the lower end of the sweet spot. Based on their recent experiences, the customers no longer perceived them as noticeably better than their competition. Therefore, they were unwilling to spend a little more to have them on their projects. Now, instead of choosing low-priced vendors and subs as a strategy for boosting margins, they were forced to work down-market because they could no longer win work at their previous price point. After the third year, it was time to call a halt to this failed experiment and return to the positive cycle of slightly higher pricing, better subs and vendors, and better value to the customer. The only trouble was, now they had some convincing to do! They had to promise customers they were going back to the way things had been, and they had to return to subs and vendors who felt burned and ask forgiveness to get back in their good graces. It was a painful two-year process of recovering their previous market position, but thankfully they had the recipe and most of the staff from the good old days there to return to grace.

Perhaps you're stuck in the negative cycle of chasing low price and scrambling to barely meet customer value expectations while grinding out a profit. This chapter has provided both the reasons for the negative cycle's existence and the recipe for breaking free from that cycle. You cannot reliably sell "best value" if you don't run every aspect of your business with a best-value philosophy because choosing the wrong options on the value curve for any part of your business will prevent you from delivering the best value to your market. Stop looking to cut corners with your costs or choosing high-end options out of loyalty. Spend what you must to get the value you need, and you can deliver (and sell!) the value your target clients need.

Delivering Value in Preconstruction and Getting Value in Return

One of the greatest values provided by contractors in the long chain of companies that bring construction projects to fruition is composed of the professional consulting services provided in preconstruction. In the often-long phase prior to construction, owners rely heavily on advice from the general contractors, who rely heavily on advice from specialty contractors to assess plan coordination, constructability issues, and value-engineering options, and to provide up-to-date accurate pricing on each element of the project. Without this information, owners would struggle to effectively budget for construction and secure sufficient funding. A practice that varies in commonness, depending on the market sector, is having multiple contractors all providing preconstruction consulting services in competition with one another. Not-so-affectionately known in the industry as *freecon*, the practice relies on the lure of competition to persuade contractors to invest more than just estimating resources, but professional consulting services, in return only for the opportunity to compete to win the project.

There are significant flaws for the owner in taking this one-sidedly beneficial approach. Most commonly, contractors forced to provide competitive free consulting services often withhold information about scope gaps or loose material specifications that they will use to justify lower pricing with a strategy of fighting for change orders later. In addition, the entire practice leads to inefficiency for contractors who must add overhead staff to preconstruction departments, which are often unable to monetize their efforts, so those costs are inevitably passed along to the owner through increased overhead. Even so, leaving all these flaws aside, freecon is such a common practice in markets like multifamily, retail, office, and other developer-driven construction areas that many contractors rarely experience any other path to winning work. I hope this strikes a nerve for you and the conversation grows because of this book, as I believe it is worth broadening the conversation about freecon to reverse this broken process in the market. However, contractors need to live in reality today and determine the best way to navigate the market.

On projects with more progressive delivery methods like design, build, and integrated project delivery, preconstruction abilities are only more valuable. WBCCs have realized the significance of strong preconstruction consulting services to their customers, regardless of delivery method, and are investing in strategies for delivering incredible customer value in precon. What differentiates them from the average, aside from a superior preconstruction product, is their willingness to secure commitments from decision-makers in return for the value they provide. Rather than providing free consulting services for months or years, only to lose in a competitive low-bid procurement process, these contractors know the value they bring to the table. They secure verbal and written commitments from their customers in return for this value.

They actively market their preconstruction skills and experience, and should a customer ask to engage their preconstruction services, they are prepared to put a price tag on the effort. They're also willing to barter in exchange for the owner stopping the competitive bidding process, limiting the number and type of competition, or being treated like the preferred contractor and given an opportunity to negotiate a deal once a bid process has completed. I'll save my critiques about procurement norms and what we can do to change them for a future publication, but for now, I will simply say that if you are a construction company subject to the norms described above, learning how to navigate the system and get credit for the value you're delivering in preconstruction can be the difference of more than 10 percent in bid-to-win rates and more than 3 percent in gross profit. You can't ignore the market's demands for top-notch preconstruction consulting, but you can convert your efforts into a solid return on investment.

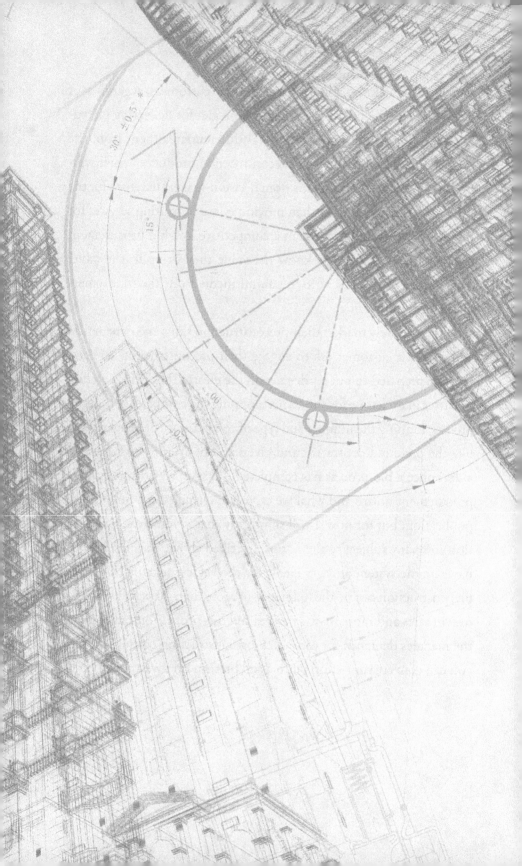

Build Real Relationships with Your Clients

It's easy to approach clients in the construction industry with a transactional mindset. Isn't that how they typically approach you? "Bid this project for us, and we might consider sitting down with you if we have any questions" is the norm, right? Real relationships—those based on a genuine liking for each other and mutual exploration of information and interests beyond the absolute task at hand—are rare for many contractors. There's nothing about the typical bid-and-wait pursuit model in construction that suggests relationships even factor into the equation for winning work. However, when I talk to most contractors about this idea, I'll often ask them if they have any clients who give them most of their work. The typical answer is, "Sure, we do." I then ask them why they think that is, to which the answer is, "Because they like us and trust us" or some variation of that theme. This simple exchange helps me illustrate that, while relationships translating into reliable work with their clients is not their norm, it is possible, and they have proof. Imagine a world in which all your projects are done with clients you have a real relationship with. What might that look like? I'll tell you. Higher win rates, better margins at the time of sale, more collaborative problem-solving, and better conflict resolution, for starters. Any relationship-first contractor will tell you that relationships are their strategic advantage. They are right, and if you're not taking this approach, you are working harder than your relationship-first peers. How do we become relationship-first contractors? Let's dig in.

Relationship-First Mindset

I will acknowledge that some clients have absolutely no interest in developing a relationship with you, and some others are prevented by internal policy from doing so. Still, they're in the minority. For GCs, most developers, architects, and owners' reps are open to building real relationships with you. For specialty contractors, the vast majority of GCs and the above list are as well. The starting point is to embrace a positive mindset about relationship development yourself. Companies are hired to build projects for other entities, but humans are the ones building projects together. You are doing the right thing for the project, the owner, your company, and your customer (if not the owner) by developing relationships with the people you will work with. It is proven that project teams that know and like one another work faster and more effectively together than a team of strangers with contracts alone binding them together.

Selfishly, your preconstruction efforts come at a great and often unrecoverable cost to your organization. It is wasteful and downright irresponsible to burn thousands of hours in estimating, budgeting, and value engineering in the pursuit of a project you have a minimal chance of winning and that, even if you won, would mean dealing with a client you might hate working with.

Embrace a mindset of building relationships through a genuine desire to work well with your clients, and be equally open to your vendors building relationships with you. With this mindset, you'll break free from the hesitancy that may keep you from enjoying the benefits of working with people you sincerely enjoy. In an interview I conducted with longtime director of purchasing at Clark Construction, Larry Stovicek, he shared a story about Clark's late owner and industry icon, Jim Clark, in which he said, "I built this company with my friends."[15] He wasn't only talking about his trusted employees but also the many trade partners with whom he had deep personal relationships. If it's good enough for Jim Clark, the founder of one of the undisputed top .01 percent general contractors on the planet, it's good enough for me.

Progression of Relationship and the Impact on Pursuit Success

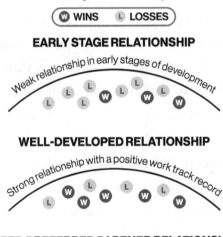

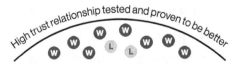

---

15   Stovicek, Larry. Interview by Chad Prinkey. Zoom call, January 26, 2023.

Seize the Opportunity

Every day you're hearing about, reading about, or even being approached by strangers who are potential clients with opportunities to bid work. Each known need in the market presents an opportunity—not only the slim opportunity to win their work, but also, much more importantly, the opportunity to create a connection. Instead of making an internal decision to bid or pass on their work and simply communicating your intent, seize the opportunity in front of you to call and introduce yourself. Tell them that you received the invite and realize you didn't know each other and wanted to remedy that by picking up the phone. Suggest a meeting between your companies to explore whether it makes sense to work together before you bid. If someone wants you to spend hours bidding their project for a one-in-ten chance of winning the project, the least they could do is take an hour to meet with you, right? When you do meet, make it clear that you're not there to talk about any specific project, but instead that you're interested in learning about them, sharing information about your company, and agreeing after the meeting whether it makes sense for you to work together. Then, if appropriate, you can discuss the merits of the project they were seeking bids for in the first place.

Right now, you are on projects with architects and engineers you don't know, GCs you are only transacting with to build the project, and owners whose only interest has been the status of their project. These people eat meals and drink coffee, and some enjoy a beer after work. Seize the opportunity to get to know these people beyond the scope of your current project and build a human connection with them. I know you have enough friends and don't have time, but if I told you that by making this simple investment, you'd save time bidding losing work to strangers and fighting with transactional customers on miserable projects that your team wishes you never took … could I change your mind?

The Path to Deep Relationships

Every now and again, you'll have a business meeting with someone with whom you connect. You share common interests, locations, friends, and more. These situations open the door for you to build deeper relationships with your clients with positive impacts on both your life and your business. Read each situation correctly, and don't overstep each person's boundaries. We are all wired differently, and with your customers, it is your job to adjust your style to how they are wired. Some people might like going to a game with you, fishing, golfing, or hunting. Others might enjoy having a coffee a few times a year, and still others would rather do none of that but might appreciate a handwritten note with personal references sometimes. Deep relationships equate to high trust, which equates to a special business relationship. When the opportunity to build a deep relationship presents itself, you'd be out of your mind not to pursue it for business reasons but for personal reasons too; friendships enrich our lives. You don't have enough friends already, I promise.

Let's say you called the construction manager from the developer you're building for right now and say, "Hey, I thought it would be good to get together and grab a coffee sometime this week. I feel like the only time we talk is about the project, and I'd like to just learn more about you and your company overall." Way to go! When you're meeting, you find out that she loves the outdoors and goes camping regularly with her family. It turns out that you do as well, and incredibly, you've both enjoyed camping at many of the same great locations. Not only does this provide great bonding material to make today's meeting a success, but it also opens the door to a human connection that provides the spark for a deeper relationship. After the meeting, you send her two maps of remote camping locations she would love and some advice for navigating them. The connection is solidifying. Two months later, after one of your OAC meetings, you ask if she's visited either. She has, and a forty-five-minute download of her best trip of the year ensues. This bonding continues over time, and the connection you've made has translated into a transparent relationship with your now best and longest-standing client.

Another consideration for building deep relationships with your client companies is to think about the many decision-makers, decision influencers, and future decision-makers on their team. Every relationship matters. To think you have a client for life because you're very close with the current VP of construction fails to consider the ways that relationship could disappear, leaving you out in the cold. Your business should build relationships all the way up and down your clients' organizational charts. This expands your business in the present, protects it in the future, and opens doors for growth you're not even thinking of today. Many current presidents and CEOs were once assistant project managers.

Set a Goal and Stick to It

I'm almost done with this lecture, I promise, but I would be remiss if I didn't give you the most important secret to follow-through. Set a goal for how much relationship development you want to do each month and stick to it. On the low end, I recommend my clients have all their PMs, estimators, and executives committed to meeting with two current or potential customers for coffee, lunch, or a beer each month. For a company with ten or twelve people in those positions, that amounts to two-hundred-plus relationship development interactions every year. The results? Smoother projects, better issue resolution, better win rates, and better margins at the time of sale. The alternative is that you can talk about it, think about it, say you should do it, and fail to follow through. The results?

Topping Out and Running Up the Score

A s any fan of college football knows, for achieving the highest possible national rank, it's not just *that* you win but also how much you win *by* that counts. Eking out a victory against a lesser opponent actually harms the winning team's chances of being top ranked. So as much as it can look like poor sportsmanship to the untrained eye, college football juggernauts must put up as many points against their opponents as they can, never taking their foot off the gas, in a practice known as running up the score. Before you judge the coaches and players for demoralizing their opponents in 55–0 routs, stop and consider that the winning team wasn't just playing today's opponent; they were also playing all the rest of the top ranked teams in action at the same time, while those who vote on weekly rankings consider which of the top teams is most qualified for the highest rankings. To finish the season at number one (and who doesn't want that?), you must play all-out every minute of every game because there is always someone right behind you doing the same who can snatch your number-one ranking out from under you. So it is in business.

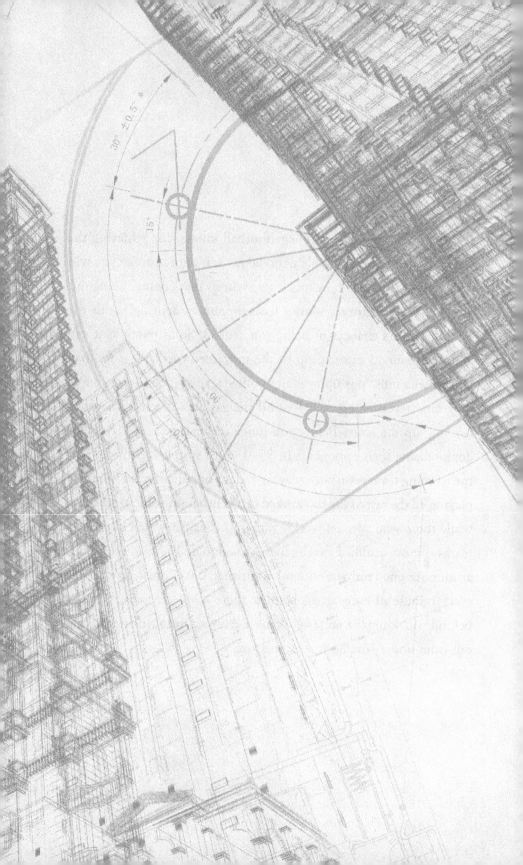

CHAPTER 22

Being Known as the Best

WBCCs are known as the best options in the markets they serve. People will do anything they can to hire the best option for their project, which they can't always do depending on pricing and availability. There is no lack of demand. Because these top companies follow the other principles laid out in this book, they have clear brand identities, operational excellence, happy customers, happy employees, high levels of consistency, and great bottom-line financial performances. Once reaching this high ground, which only the top 2 percent of construction industry companies ever reach, it's tempting to take success for granted and take one's foot off the gas. It is imperative to resist that temptation and continue the disciplines that got you to the top. Always run your business like there is stiff competition giving everything they've got to climb to the top and take your number-one ranking.

What does it take to extend your advantage? Believe it or not, the answer is usually mastering the fundamentals and being consistent. Too many companies get confused about the fundamentals, lose their focus, and blow their lead. There are some pitfalls to avoid once you've become a top 2 percent construction company. These points are relevant for those still climbing to the top, too, but they're particularly important to those who may feel they've achieved top ranking already.

CHAPTER 23

Pitfalls of Top Performers

Putting the Numbers over Much More Important Things

This destructive phenomenon can be seen frequently by observing the likes of publicly traded companies that have become slaves to their quarterly earnings reports and delivering shareholder value. Most construction companies are not publicly traded, but many top-performing companies reach the top and fall victim to the same thinking that dooms public firms. This pitfall occurs when the company becomes so obsessed with the numbers they forget about the culture and the people driving all their success. Key employees who have delivered incredible results over the years have their compensation plans cut or their titles reduced, or are eliminated from the company in the name of cutting overhead while the market and the rest of the company mourn the loss of a valuable mentor and partner. The company team-building-event budget is cut while the culture slowly erodes into a watered-down version of what it once was. An obsession with dragging another two points of GP out of an already strong production staff hurts relationships with vendors and customers, making it harder to run a successful, profitable project.

The companies guilty of putting the numbers over much more important things fail to recognize that, for most of their numbers-driven decisions, the repercussions are more expensive than it would have been to leave things as they were. The cure was worse than the disease. And all this penny-wise-and-pound-foolish behavior diminishes their advantage over the rest of the pack, reducing their lead and putting them in a position to be overtaken. The employees who were marginalized and disenfranchised go to the competition, even if there's a noncompete, and bring the secret-sauce recipe with them. The vendors who get burned start actively helping their other customers with better service and pricing to level the score against the unfair competition. And those long-standing clients, feeling less loyalty because of the way they were treated on the last project, open the door for new competition for the first time in a long while.

The next thing they know, the competition is much closer to them than before. The momentum has shifted, and they're fighting to stay in the lead. And once momentum shifts, it can be impossible to recover. Don't believe me? Ask Blockbuster about Netflix.

Playing Not to Lose Rather Than Playing to Win

I'm realizing that if you know nothing about football, this chapter might be annoying, and if that's you, I'm very sorry about it, but you have to trust me on this ... the analogies are too relevant not to use. When a team has a lead in the fourth quarter, it's common to see a defense begin to play a prevent-defense formation. This is when the eleven-person defensive unit sends seven or eight of their players far away from the line of scrimmage to prevent a long pass from being completed. It is the most conservative defensive formation, and the logic behind it stems from the thought that the offense, needing urgently to score to reduce their deficit, will throw the ball long on every play, and the defense only must keep them out of the end zone. What every fan of a team who has deployed this tactic and blown a significant lead has seen is this ultraconservative strategy is deeply flawed because it allows far too much space underneath the deep coverage of the defense for the offense to move down the field one chunk at a time until suddenly, they're just yards away from scoring. Coaches are responsible for calling the defensive plays, and when you see your team in the prevent formation while there is still time on the clock, you know that your coach is not playing to win. Instead, he's playing not to lose.

The strategy the team uses to build that big lead is seldom an ultraconservative, prevent-defense approach. It isn't until the lead is built that many coaches throw out what's working and go into a shell to protect their lead. Why don't they keep doing the things that created success in the first place? The answer is their mindset. When these teams don't have a lead, they play like there is nothing to lose. Once they have the lead, they fear losing what they think they have. But they don't have anything until the game is over! If teams keep on thinking like there is nothing to lose until it's over, the strategy wins the game, not to keep from losing it.

Overconfidence

It's great to have confidence in yourself and your company. Among other great things, confidence attracts employees and customers to your brand and leads to positive morale. If you want to become a WBCC, confidence is a must. However, crossing the line from confidence into overconfidence is a recipe for downfall. The line can be difficult to see, especially for the one crossing the line, but it's there. The trick is to avoid becoming enamored with yourselves and letting your ego tell you that you're so special and different that you're immune to problems. It requires sobriety and the awareness that if your organization could climb to the top, others are capable as well. And there's the complexity of the line between confidence and overconfidence. You must be capable of simultaneously extolling the value and benefits of working with your company, while recognizing that there remains considerable room for improvement and innovation. The moment you think you've made it, the backslide begins.

Wait ... so can you celebrate your accomplishments without backsliding? Yes.

One thing WBCCs do to combat overconfidence is to define success as acting the right way daily from top to bottom in the organization. It's not as much about the big project you won or the top profit quarter you had as it is about the admirable actions taken by the people who contribute to those outcomes every day. They celebrate more often, recognize more people deeper into the organization, and enjoy better employee engagement. To the point of this chapter, however, the most important thing that happens when you celebrate your team doing the right thing is you set them up to refocus on winning every day because the win comes as action. They follow the leadership examples set by people like Bill Walsh and John Wooden, believing that if the team does the right things consistently, makes the right choices, and does the hard work, they'll be holding the trophy at the end of the season. But today it doesn't matter if your team won the trophy last season, does it? The thing that earned you the trophy last season was doing the right thing day in and day out. That is the definition of winning. Trophies are symbols that reinforce the right action, not proof that you've somehow made it.

Another risk of overconfidence for a top 2 percent construction company is allowing the demand for your services to cause you to take more work than you can handle. Construction companies that believe they can do as much work as the market can throw their way will find themselves on a backslide. Remember, the thing that puts more construction companies out of business than any other is taking on more work than they can perform and getting themselves in trouble with cash. There are notable examples of this that underscore the risks associated with trying to handle too many (especially large) projects. Even if you aren't in the financial jeopardy over taking on too much work, the strains caused by an intolerable workload will lead to lower morale and quality issues and will eventually tarnish your reputation. Even the top 2 percent companies would do well to focus on the discipline lessons from the "Maintain a Healthy Diet" chapter.

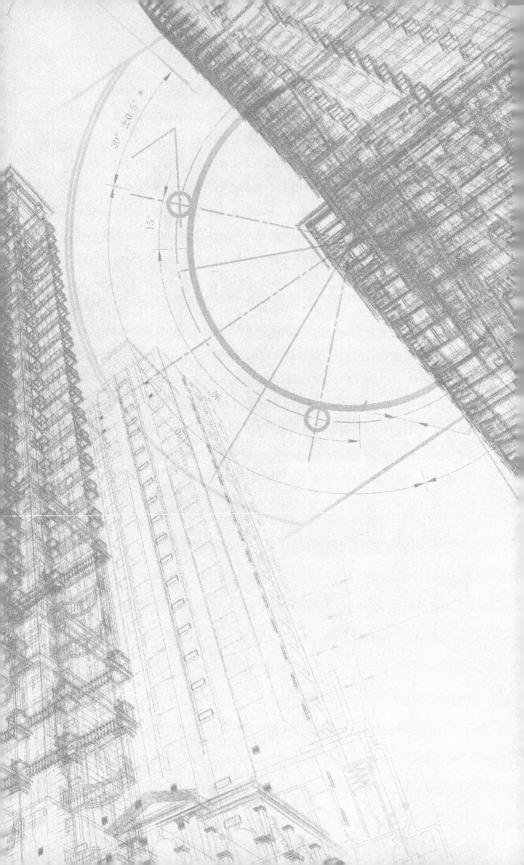

CHAPTER 24

Strategies for Running Up the Score

In business, the game is never over, so you can never secure the final win. All you can do is define what winning means to your team repeatedly and play each day for that win. There's no sense in protecting a lead in a game that never ends. Instead, always run up the score! I'm not saying that WBCCs are universally aggressive in their business strategies. Some are, and others are more conservative. I am saying that when they get to the top, they stick to their knitting and keep doing the things that made them successful. What they don't do is become more and more conservative as they reach success. They continue to define what winning looks like, and they play for the win by extending their lead on the pack. Below are some examples of things WBCCs do to run up the score.

Create Internal Efficiencies

Construction companies often complain about their more successful competition by saying, "They can afford to lose money and buy jobs we can't." Having been exposed to their top-tier competitors over the years, I've come to find that statement isn't 100 percent accurate. The less successful competitors don't know how they're doing it, so they've made up a story that helps them sleep at night. A side note: It doesn't make you better as a company or a person to explain away your underperformance with fairy tales that help you feel better about yourself. In the case of the WBCC versus their competition, it would be more accurate to say, "They have created such efficient operations that their costs are lower than ours, even though we're smaller than them. Therefore, when they want to beat our price, they can easily do it, making better margin at that lower price than we do at our target price."

So how do you create internal efficiencies in your business? It starts by finding your inefficiencies. As it can be difficult to spot your problems from inside your business, the best course of action here is often to rely on inviting outsiders into your business for an assessment. Your peer community, a consultant, and even your newest employees from outside your company can look at your business with the fresh eyes needed to spot inefficiencies. The most common solutions to create efficiency revolve around process improvements and new technologies. As for new technology, innovations happen in the building industry all the time, and WBCCs know the difference between becoming infatuated with new innovations and using innovations strategically to drive business results.

To unlock major efficiency gains, sometimes a major investment is necessary. One mechanical contractor could see that their lack of ability to control conditions in the field was leading to significant manpower-productivity losses. In addition, assembling their systems alongside other trades in real time was causing mistakes and leading to rework and back charges. As a part of a mechanical contracting peer community, they had seen a noncompetitive mechanical contractor in another state who invested in an off-site fabrication facility to address just such challenges. The efficiency gains the peer company experienced were significant enough to motivate my client to make the same investment in their business. The $4 million facility and equipment were paid for by the efficiency gains only after three years, and the resulting boost in profitability was there to stay, allowing them to really run up the score in their market.

Sometimes efficiency gains come in very simple forms. One client, for example, a design/build CM firm, could complete their projects 10 percent faster consistently while improving quality by implementing an internal and external meeting structure that provided staff with more high-quality, timely feedback that nearly eliminated late revisions. They got that idea from their consultant (me, in this case), who, with their outsider perspective, was able to easily see the inefficiency created by holding too few low-quality meetings during design and the subsequent mad dash to the finish, as major design elements had to be reworked at the eleventh hour. This new meeting structure added a nominal amount of time earlier and saved massive time and stress late in design. When they made this change, the overwhelming reaction from the group was, "How were we not doing this all along?" Multiply these types of efficiency gains across your organization, and the results can be incredible.

Setting a New Bar

In his book *With Winning in Mind*, Olympian Lanny Bassham describes the low point of his Olympic career as the time back in the Olympic village later in the day after winning his first gold medal in riflery.[16] Yes, you read that correctly. He felt the lowest after the adrenaline and pride wore off from the gold medal ceremony. The reason? He had lost his goal. When his wife helped him to come to this realization, Bassham took swift action by creating a new goal to strive for, and his sense of joy and meaning returned.

When they're climbing the proverbial mountain trying to achieve their vision, construction companies are united by a shared experience, striving toward a common and inspiring goal. Following the WBCC System, I am confident that you and your team will feel this sense of passion and unity. It's extremely rewarding, and I'm excited for you! However, once you reach the top of the mountain, you must create a new target for your team to pursue, or you'll risk losing a sense of meaning while complacency creeps in. When I talk to some construction executives about this concept, it hits them as almost depressing. Some say, "It's never enough!"

Of all the passages you've read thus far, this one may be the most important, so read it and reread it until it really sinks in. *The successful striving toward the goal, not the attainment of the goal, is the definition of success.* What's it all for? In the largest possible sense, what are you trying to accomplish by building a great business? Why are you reading this book? At the core of it for all of us is the same motivation to be happy. That's why we strive to begin with: we believe we'll be happy when we get to the top of the mountain. However—and this is important to wrap your head around—the thing that actually makes people happy is *not* reaching their goals, but rather it is the sense of pride and self-worth that comes with doing hard things at a high level. Your actions and not your outcomes are actually what make you happy. It's precisely why great teams striving to reach the

---

16 Lanny Bassham, *With Winning in Mind: The Mental Management System* (USA: Mental Management Systems, 1995), 18.

pinnacle are at such peril of becoming complacent once they have nothing to strive for. To experience the most satisfaction in our lives, people need to feel like they are doing something good and important. At work, giving people something to work toward that inspires them brings that out in them. If you don't triple your size (you double it), or open five new markets (you open four), or achieve five times your profits (you triple them), or any of the other things you outlined in your vision, but you and your team played at their highest level and did their best along the way, you won.

I recommend three-to-five-year visions, annual business plans, and quarterly benchmarks. Depending on the timeframe for your vision, you should be redrafting it with select team members every three to five years to provide an inspirational target to build toward. There should be a detailed annual business plan connecting to the vision and representing exciting progress for every department in the business, and every quarter we should have that annual plan broken down into benchmarks that will show we're on track for the annual plan and the vision. I think you can deviate from the outline I've provided if you remember the purpose: to have a constant source of inspiration in place for you and your team to be at your best every day.

Being Incredibly Generous

For construction company owners and executives making strong profits in a tough and fickle industry, the temptation is to pay themselves handsomely when times are good because the economy can shift and create tough times around the corner. Owners and execs deserve to enjoy their financial success—no argument there. However, the companies that consistently maintain their position at the top can extend their advantage in the market not by paying the owners and execs more money, but by being generous with their people, their clients, and their communities. Exciting bonuses, company picnics, improved benefits programs, better facilities, training programs, and more are all ways of using generosity to your advantage with your people.

Employees who feel more appreciated are significantly more likely to give their best to the company and stay for the long haul. Clients remember that five-star client appreciation event you hosted for them and the relationships that you developed when they award their next project.

Charitable giving to causes that matter to your employees and clients creates immeasurable goodwill. Using your prosperity to do good for people around you comes back to your company many times over.

Doing Good in the Industry

As your company reaches new heights of financial performance, opportunities to invest in the greater construction industry will present themselves. Fear-based, small-minded company owners might think, "Why would I want to help the whole industry? I want to keep the benefits of my success just for me." They'd be missing the thought that, as JFK said, "A rising tide lifts all boats" and that by contributing to the industry, goodwill is created, even with your competitors.

Yes, being on good terms with your competition is possible and even preferable. Investing in the local training centers or technical schools not only helps prepare more young people to enter the industry but also puts you squarely in the sights of those future candidates for internships and careers with your company.

Staying Humble

Top-performing hedge fund manager, billionaire, and accomplished author Ray Dalio likes to remind himself, "I know far too little compared to that which I need to know."[17] He knows that being a forever student is the only path to maintaining an advantage. This self-effacing statement is a consistent reminder that staying hungry for improvement is rooted in humility and a belief in a need for improvement. I can think of many conversations I've had with construction executives who tell me, in one way or another, that they don't need to improve at this point. Yet, it rarely sounds like that. Instead, it sounds like: "We're in a good spot right now, so we're not trying to do anything to rock the boat" and "We were the model company in our peer group, so I don't think we'd get enough value from our involvement." The decision to stop improving is music to your competitors' ears.

Executives should seek audiences with leaders from other construction companies they admire to get guidance. All leaders should undergo 360-degree evaluations regularly from the people they work for, around, and above. In the Excellence in Estimating section, every project should receive an after-action review (AAR) in which candid feedback from customers, subcontractors, design team members, and all departments is shared and explored for meaningful improvements. Efforts should be made to hire people who are smarter than your smartest people; listen to their feedback about your business early and often. And so on …

If you're at the top of your game, good for you! Now stay humble, remember where you came from, and recognize that being better than your competition isn't the same as being as good as you can be.

---

17   Dalio, Ray. *Principles: Life and Work.* Simon & Schuster, 2017.

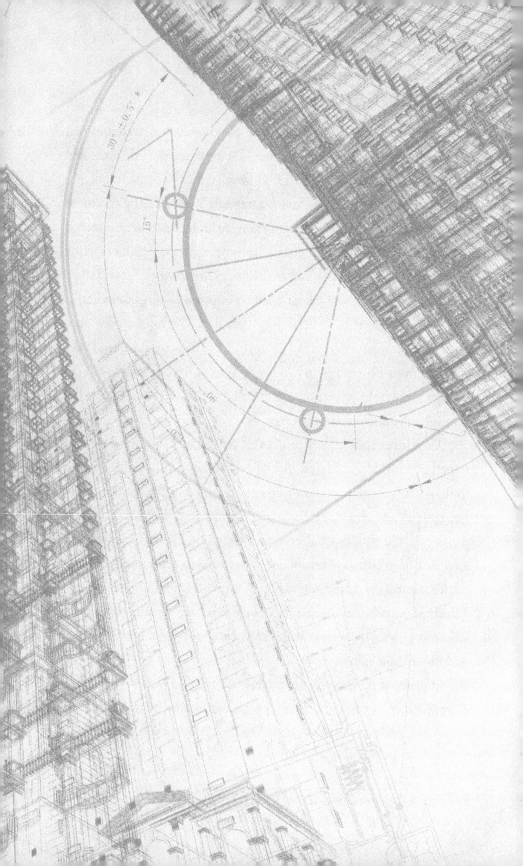

You Will Encounter Obstacles and Pushback— Execute Anyway

We take risks knowing that risk will sometimes result in failure. But without the possibility of failure, there is no possibility of success.

—TIM COOK

On your path to becoming a top-2-percent company, you'll face significant obstacles to implementing the WBCC System. In the one-hundred-plus consulting engagements we've had with contractors, these principles have never been flawless in our clients' businesses. Still, our clients have been overwhelmingly successful at becoming top-2-percent contractors despite their obstacles, with fewer than 10 percent of our engagements falling short of what we'd mutually describe as a success. In every single successful case, commitment is the key.

These contractors are unwilling to accept the status quo any longer, and they do whatever it takes to become great. That sounds like you, right? You're a kick-ass construction executive that's not going to accept mediocrity! Good. You'll need that confidence.

Here's a list of the obstacles you may face along the way:

1. Resistance to change

2. Toxic or misfit key employees

3. Personal financial steps back

4. Lack of accountability

5. Subversion of the effort from within

6. You

As we cover this final principle, our chapter will show how to identify and overcome each obstacle. It won't be easy, but if you're committed to uncommon success, you must be willing to take uncommon action.

Change Management

One owner spent a week away from her business, thinking about his personal goals and how the business needed to change to meet her goals. It was a great choice, and she returned with incredible clarity about how she wanted things to run. The first few steps of her new plan relied heavily on department managers to take on more responsibility for creating processes in their departments. In his first meeting with the department heads to roll out these changes, she started the meeting by saying, "Everyone is going to need to step up or get out of the way for someone who will!" Unknowingly, she struck the wrong note for her team, which was working as hard as it was and had always been positive and supportive. That comment left a mark, and the team mounted a silent resistance to the change, joining in their opposition to the newly energized tyrant they were seeing before them. It took months to figure out what was holding back the changes, and when she finally did, it exploded into outright conflict.

I was brought in to help repair the rift with team building, for which I used a one-day retreat program based on the Five Behaviors of a Team. The retreat showed that the team felt attacked by how the owner approached them. They felt they had been much closer to the day-to-day business than the owner and had no opportunity to voice their opinions about what needed improvement and how to do it. They felt the owner insinuated that they hadn't stepped up a million times before. It created a breakdown in trust and communication and a lack of commitment to the owner's initiatives. With that on the table, the owner could see things from her team's perspective and empathize with their position. Instead of pushing her own agenda, the owner invited the team to join her in developing the vision for the company. The funny thing is, like the owner had initially, the team ended up prioritizing process development as the first step as well. With this personal buy-in, they had their processes in place in record-breaking time.

This story illustrates how deciding what changes must occur means nothing if you can't effectively manage that change into the organization. People don't react well to feeling threatened, ignored, marginalized, and pressed to the breaking point. Driving change alone is a painful, lonely process littered with setbacks that will leave you wondering why you even try. Unless you're a solopreneur, you need your good people to help you with change. You must involve them in the process in a positive way. It starts with having shared CSD, so pay extra attention to that principle in the book. With CSD in place, the team can confidently communicate that they are all rowing in the same direction and that the right decision for the team aligns with our CSD. Then it becomes less about winning people over or arguing your point and more about letting the best solution become clear, regardless of where the idea originates.

Hard Decisions

As you develop your CSD together, you may identify irreconcilable differences with one or more team members. A person may either overtly or covertly oppose the group's decisions. Often, this is an employee with long tenure and hard-earned opinions not up for debate. Decisions on CSD must incorporate everyone's feedback and ensure the entire team feels heard. Disagreement is normal, and the team need not agree with every decision made, but it needs to unite behind the decisions, regardless, and support them 100 percent. The final call belongs to the CEO, often the owner, who must practice the attributes of being a Well Built Leader when making the hard decision.

When team members cannot see their way to supporting the CSD for the company, we must be ready to encourage them to leave or let them go. They don't like where this train is going anyway, so it'd be best for everyone if they got off before we're too far down the line. If they are allowed to remain on the team, they'll undermine morale and become a distraction. Worse, if they are allowed to pull in the opposite direction from the rest of the team, they'll knock you off course, and you'll lose people's hearts and minds from pursuing your CSD altogether. I've seen many good people quit their jobs after losing faith in leadership. Good people will not suffer being surrounded by not-good people for long. You must be ready to make the hard decisions, which sometimes means saying goodbye to longtime friends and employees.

Other hard decisions, like saying no to work we didn't want, spending the money to open that new division, or closing the under-performing division must also be made. Once you've built the plan to implement the WBCC Systems, you must have the courage to follow through.

Disciplined Execution

Few things of any value come easily or quickly. Most require consistent hard work and discipline. As you set out to become a WBCC, know in advance that it will suck before it gets fun. Nobody likes the discom-fort of lifting weights or sustained cardio activity, but everybody likes the results. Those who have developed strong exercise habits have even managed to take some joy in the discomfort, knowing what results are to come. Perhaps you can achieve that mental state while making changes in your construction business. Whether the investment is time, money, or energy, expect it to be harder than you think, and be ready to see it through. Don't be the developer who starts a project and leaves it as a giant, empty hole in the ground. See it through, but select your initiatives carefully so you can handle it.

Accountability

This is a word that gets thrown around a lot. *Webster's Dictionary* defines accountability as the quality or state of being accountable, especially an obligation to accept responsibility or to account for one's actions.[18] I think that's right. Being accountable is a personal standard.

Accountable people can be counted on to do their best at what they're expected to do and never point the finger at anyone but themselves. Taking accountability happens when an accountable person calls themselves on the carpet for failing to meet the standard. It is always followed by an action plan for preventing the miss in the future, and asking for help is an acceptable action plan. Being held accountable is necessary when unaccountable people do not meet standards, which normally has consequences, such as dismissal from a project or the team altogether. You want a team full of accountable people who can be trusted to execute most of the time. With a team like this, there will sometimes be instances where individuals will take accountability for a missed standard, but you'll work through the problems together and prevent the same issue in the future. If you find you're surrounded by unaccountable people, you'll constantly need to hold people accountable. This fraught state never holds up for long, and you'll either give up on the people or on disciplined execution. Want an accountable team? Set the standard. In every situation I've ever seen, teams lacking in accountability have leaders who are not accountable themselves. They don't respond to their emails or hit deadlines themselves. Be accountable, and you'll raise the bar for everyone. Then, refuse to accept unaccountable behavior. You need a team of people who are accountable and periodically must take accountability, and who must rarely be held accountable by others.

---

18 "Accountability." Merriam-Webster.com Dictionary. https://www.merriam-webster.com/dictionary/accountability. Accessed February 20, 2023.

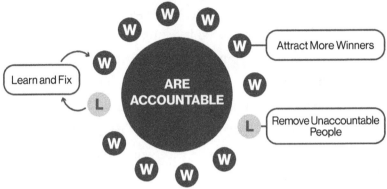

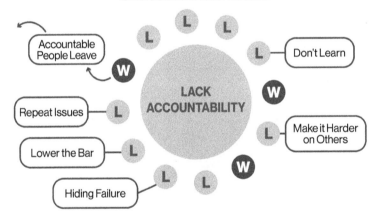

Enjoy the Journey

Becoming a top-2-percent contractor won't occur overnight. It will take many years, depending on where you're starting from. Having a compelling vision in mind is great fuel for your personal fires of motivation, but remember the wise words, "It's not the destination, it's the journey." You cannot wait until you're a top-2-percent contractor to be happy with and proud of your company. If you do, you'll never get there. People who are unhappy with and not proud of their companies don't have the confidence in them to invest in becoming great. If you are smaller than you want, making less than you want, producing lower quality than you want, or not as good a place to work as you want, the definition of success is taking positive action every day to become better. Real happiness comes from acting in a way that makes you feel proud. It feels good to know you're doing the right thing for your business. Things that make us feel proud of ourselves aren't a lot of fun in the moment but have a long-term payoff. Becoming a better contractor should feel a lot like hard work, followed by pride. Soak in that positivity, and enjoy the process of moving toward greatness.

ACKNOWLEDGMENTS

Well Built was made entirely possible by the construction company owners and executives who chose to bring me in to help their teams. You are my friends and my inspiration. Thank you for treating me like a part of your family. I hope you know I think of you as a part of mine.

I'm extremely fortunate to have many people conspiring to help me succeed for a long time.

My parents, Jim and Toni, thank you for raising me to pursue what makes me happy and to let the money figure itself out. I'm proud to be a reflection of each of you. My big brothers, Todd and Troy, have been my role models for my entire life. Thank you for guiding the way with your bold action and deep loyalty for those you love.

My wife, Lindsey, you can't possibly know how much your constant support makes me believe in myself. If you trust me like you do, I must be doing okay. Thank you for being my friend, my partner, and my cheerleader to face the toughest challenges of my life. My kids, Liam, Aaron, and Mason, give my efforts purpose. Thank you for your unconditional love, for brightening every day, and for being exactly who each of you are. You are great kids and if you listen to your family, you'll become amazing adults.

Finally, thank you to the Well Built Consulting team. Working alongside you to create positive change for our amazing clients is a truly humbling experience. Your care and expertise are second to none and I feel lucky to share this company with each of you. Thanks in advance to all future team members who will join our cause, challenge us, and make us better.

As a business coach and consultant, Chad has successfully developed nearly two hundred meaningful client relationships in the building industry by delivering real results and maintaining trust since 2008. Over that time, he has been incredibly fortunate to work with some of the best companies in the construction industry, many of whom inspired this book.

In 2021, Chad founded Well Built Consulting to bring together a team of people who are dedicated to improving the lives of the individuals who have chosen a career in the building industry by improving the great companies that are committed to doing the same. The Well Built Consulting team works relentlessly on behalf of companies with a desire to be the best they can be.

Chad is an entertainer and performer by nature and by training. He relishes opportunities to speak to groups and move people. He lives in Baltimore County, Maryland, with his wife, Lindsey, their three sons, and two black labs. They love the outdoors and have a cabin in north central Pennsylvania that serves as a family retreat and amateur fly-fishing lodge.

We're eager to connect with you! For feedback or questions about the book, please email us at booksupport@wellbuiltconsulting.com. Stay updated on our insights, newsletters, and other construction-industry-specific content by visiting www.wellbuiltconsulting.com and following Chad and Well Built Construction Consulting on LinkedIn.

Well Built Construction Consulting specializes in building better construction businesses through strategic plan development and execution support. Our amazing team can advise your business on every topic in this book. Chad and the rest of our dynamic team are passionate about speaking to construction teams and association groups on topics such as leadership and management, organizational development, team dynamics, change management, innovation, and more.

Check out the podcast, *The Morning Huddle Construction Show*, to hear about how Chad and his guests are advancing the construction community through meaningful and informative conversation at www.themorninghuddleconstructionshow.com.

You can also sign up for Topping Out—the newsletter for construction owners and executives by visiting www.wellbuiltconsulting.com/toppingout to receive regular updates, advice, and insight on creating your own Well Built company.

Interested in working together? Contact us at admin@wellbuilt-consulting.com to explore how we can work together. We're excited to hear from you and embark on this journey together!